Wisdom of the East

The Bhagavad-Gita is the timeless epic of the Hindu faith. The simple, vivid message is a daily inspiration in the lives of millions throughout the world and has been so for countless generations.

The powerful, beautiful scripture is part poem, part prose—translated here into clear, meaningful English by the brilliant contemporary novelist Christopher Isherwood and his teacher, Swami Prabhavananda. The present translators have tried to present the Bhagavad-Gita in all its aspects, combining the beauties of distinguished verse and prose, scholarship and philosophical interpretation.

This illuminating translation is designed to bring the Bhagavad-Gita closer to the ordinary, perplexed man and woman of today. The noted author, Aldous Huxley, has contributed the brilliant introduction.

There is added at the end of this book an account of the influence on Gandhi of THE SONG OF GOD, taken from the Signet Key Book, GANDHI, HIS LIFE AND MESSAGE FOR THE WORLD by Louis Fischer.

THIS VERSION OF THE BHAGAVAD-GITA IS A REPRINT OF THE ORIGINAL HARDCOVER EDITION PUBLISHED BY HARPER & BROTHERS.

The Mentor Religious Classics

The Teachings of the Compassionate Buddha
edited by E. A. Burtt
The basic texts, early discourses, the Dhammapada, and later writings of Buddhism. (#MD131—50¢)

The Upanishads: Breath of the Eternal
The wisdom of the Hindu mystics, translated by Swami Prabhavananda and Frederick Manchester. (#MD194—50¢)

The Way of Life: Tao Tê Ching *by Lao Tzu*
A new translation by R. B. Blakney of a masterpiece of ancient Chinese wisdom. (#MD129—50¢)

The Meaning of the Glorious Koran: An Explanatory Translation by Mohammed Marmaduke Pickthall
The complete sacred book of Mohammedanism, translated with reverence and scholarship. (#MT223—75¢)

The Song of God:

BHAGAVAD-GITA

TRANSLATED BY

Swami Prabhavananda

AND

Christopher Isherwood

WITH AN INTRODUCTION BY ALDOUS HUXLEY

A MENTOR RELIGIOUS CLASSIC
Published by THE NEW AMERICAN LIBRARY

*This MENTOR edition
has been printed by the permission of Marcel Rodd,
the original publisher.*

FIRST PRINTING, FEBRUARY, 1954
EIGHTH PRINTING, MAY, 1961

*The Song of God: Bhagavad-Gita is published in
England by Phoenix House Ltd.*

MENTOR TRADEMARK REG. U.S. PAT. OFF. AND FOREIGN COUNTRIES
REGISTERED TRADEMARK——MARCA REGISTRADA
HECHO EN CHICAGO, U.S.A.

*MENTOR BOOKS are published by
The New American Library of World Literature, Inc.
501 Madison Avenue, New York 22, New York*

PRINTED IN THE UNITED STATES OF AMERICA

To the memory of

SWAMI TURIYANANDA

who was regarded by his master

SRI RAMAKRISHNA

as a perfect embodiment of
that renunciation which is taught in the

BHAGAVAD-GITA

Those who wish to learn in greater detail about the teachings contained in this book are advised to communicate with the Secretary, The Vedanta Society of Southern California, 1946 Vedanta Place, Hollywood 28, California.

There is a record of readings from the BHAGAVAD-GITA available from Folkways Record Service Corporation, 117 West 46th Street, New York, New York.

Contents

BHAGAVAD-GITA

Translators' Preface

NOWADAYS, it is becoming fashionable to translate the world's great books into some form of Basic English, or everyday speech. The Gita does not easily lend itself to such treatment. The Sanskrit in which it is written differs radically from modern English. It is compressed and telegraphic. It abounds in exact philosophical and religious terms. Its frame of reference is a system of cosmology unfamiliar to western thought. And indeed, it would be hard to evolve any uniform English style, modern or ancient, in which the Gita could be satisfactorily rendered. For the Gita, regarded simply as a piece of literature, is not a unity. It has several aspects, several distinct tones of voice. Let us consider each of them in turn.

First, the Gita may be regarded as part of an epic poem. It is all in verse. The first chapter is pure epic, continuing in the mood of the Mahabharata itself. The shouting of warriors, the neighing of horses and the outlandish names of chieftains are still sounding in our ears as the dialogue between Krishna and Arjuna begins. To translate this epic prologue as though it belonged to the philosophical discourse which follows would be to cut the Gita right out of its historical setting and deprive it of its vivid local colour.

Then, again, the Gita is an exposition of Vedanta philosophy, based upon a very definite picture of the universe. It is no use trying to disregard this fact for fear of alienating the western reader. The translator who uses 'reassuring' topical equivalents, and twists the meaning of the Sanskrit terms, may think he is building a bridge between two systems of thought, when actually he is reducing both of them to nonsense. We have tried to explain the cosmology of the

Gita, as briefly as possible, in an appendix. Certain basic and much-used words, such as *Brahman, Atman, Prakriti* and the *gunas,* have been kept in Sanskrit, for the same reason. Precise English equivalents are lacking; and every book on philosophy or science must have a defined terminology. No one would write about physics and avoid using the word 'electron,' just because it does not occur in everyday speech.

The Gita is also prophetic. Like the Vision of Isaiah and the Psalms of David, it contains ecstatic mystical utterances about the nature and attributes of God. These are poetry, and demand poetic expression. The diction must try to correspond to the inspiration. Ordinary prose will render them flat and boring.

Finally, the Gita is a gospel. Its essential message is timeless. In words which belong to no one language, race or epoch, incarnate God speaks to man, His friend. Here, the translator must forget all about Vedanta philosophy and Sanskrit terms; all about India and the West, Krishna and Arjuna, past and future. He must aim at the utmost simplicity.

That is why we have translated the Gita in a variety of styles, partly prose, partly verse. There is, of course, no justification for this experiment in the text itself. The transitions from one style to another are quite arbitrary. They can be judged from one standpoint only: have we made the book more readable?

Extremely literal translations of the Gita already exist. We have aimed, rather, at an interpretation. Here is one of the greatest religious documents of the world: let us not approach it too pedantically, as an archaic text which must be jealously preserved by university professors. It has something to say, urgently, to every one of us. We have to extract that message from the terseness of the original Sanskrit, and here the great classical commentators can help us. In making this translation, three of them have been consulted throughout—Shankara, Sridhara Swami and Madhusudana Saraswati. Wishing to avoid bulky footnotes, we have incorporated their explanations in our English version. Sri Aurobindo Ghose's masterly *Essays on the Gita* have also been helpful. Nevertheless, our work is not a paraphrase. Except in a very few difficult passages, it faithfully follows the original.

We have allowed overselves one small liberty. The Gita is sprinkled with epithets. Krishna is called 'Govinda,' 'Slayer of Madhu,' 'Keshava,' etc. Arjuna is addressed as 'Consumer of the foe,' 'Son of Kunti,' 'Descendant of Bharata,' 'Son of Pritha,' and much else. We have kept a few of these, in the opening chapters, to create 'atmosphere.' Later, they are mostly omitted, unless they seem effective for purely literary reasons. Their repetition is apt to grow very tiresome.

In conclusion, we have to thank our friends, Margaret Adams Kiskadden and Aldous Huxley, for their help, frank criticism and warm encouragement. The final draft of our translation owes them much, perhaps its very existence.

Introduction

MORE THAN twenty-five centuries have passed since that which has been called the Perennial Philosophy was first committed to writing; and in the course of those centuries it has found expression, now partial, now complete, now in this form, now in that, again and again. In Vedanta and Hebrew prophecy, in the Tao Teh King and the Platonic dialogues, in the

Gospel according to St. John and Mahayana theology, in Plotinus and the Areopagite, among the Persian Sufis and the Christian mystics of the Middle Ages and the Renaissance—the Perennial Philosophy has spoken almost all the languages of Asia and Europe and has made use of the terminology and traditions of every one of the higher religions. But under all this confusion of tongues and myths, of local histories and particularist doctrines, there remains a Highest Common Factor, which is the Perennial Philosophy in what may be called its chemically pure state. This final purity can never, of course, be expressed by any verbal statement of the philosophy, however undogmatic that statement may be, however deliberately syncretistic. The very fact that it is set down at a certain time by a certain writer, using this or that language, automatically imposes a certain sociological and personal bias on the doctrines so formulated. It is only in the act of contemplation, when words and even personality are transcended, that the pure state of the Perennial Philosophy can actually be known. The records left by those who have known it in this way make it abundantly clear that all of them, whether Hindu, Buddhist, Hebrew, Taoist, Christian or Mohammedan, were attempting to describe the same essentially indescribable Fact.

The original scriptures of most religions are poetical and unsystematic. Theology, which generally takes the form of a reasoned commentary on the parables and aphrosims of the scriptures, tends to make its appearance at a later stage of religious history. The Bhagavad–Gita occupies an intermediate position between scripture and theology; for it combines the poetical qualities of the first with the clear cut methodicalness of the second. The book may be described, writes Ananda K. Coomaraswamy in his admirable *Hinduism and Buddhism,* 'as a compendium of the whole Vedic doctrine to be found in the earlier Vedas, Brahmanas and Upanishads, and being therefore the basis of all the later developments, it can be regarded as the focus of all Indian religion.' But this 'focus of Indian religion' is also one of the clearest and most comprehensive summaries of the Perennial Philosophy ever to have been made. Hence its enduring value, not only for Indians, but for all mankind.

At the core of the Perennial Philosophy we find four fundamental doctrines.

First: the phenomenal world of matter and of individualized consciousness—the world of things and animals and men and even gods—is the manifestation of a Divine Ground within which all partial realities have their being, and apart from which they would be nonexistent.

Second: human beings are capable not merely of knowing *about* the Divine Ground by inference; they can also realize its existence by a direct intuition, superior to discursive reasoning. This immediate knowledge unites the knower with that which is known.

Third: man possesses a double nature, a phenomenal ego and an eternal Self, which is the inner man, the spirit, the spark of divinity within the soul. It is possible for a man, if he so desires, to identify himself with the spirit and therefore with the Divine Ground, which is of the same or like nature with the spirit.

Fourth: man's life on earth has only one end and purpose: to identify himself with his eternal Self and so to come to unitive knowledge of the Divine Ground. (Brahman)

In Hinduism the first of these four doctrines is stated in the most categorical terms. The Divine

Ground is Brahman, whose creative, sustaining and transforming aspects are manifested in the Hindu trinity. A hierarchy of manifestations connects inanimate matter with man, gods, High Gods and the undifferentiated Godhead beyond.

In Mahayana Buddhism the Divine Ground is called Mind or the Pure Light of the Void, the place of the High Gods is taken by the Dhyani-Buddhas.

Similar conceptions are perfectly compatible with Christianity and have in fact been entertained, explicitly or implicitly, by many Catholic and Protestant mystics, when formulating a philosophy to fit facts observed by super-rational intuition. Thus, for Eckhart and Ruysbroeck, there is an Abyss of Godhead underlying the Trinity, just as Brahman underlies Brahma, Vishnu and Shiva. Suso has even left a diagrammatic picture of the relations subsisting between Godhead, triune God and creatures. In this very curious and interesting drawing a chain of manifestation connects the mysterious symbol of the Divine Ground with the three Persons of the Trinity, and the Trinity in turn is connected in a descending scale with angels and human beings. These last, as the drawing vividly shows, may make one of two choices. They can either lead the life of the outer man, the life of separative selfhood; in which case they are lost (for, in the words of the Theologia Germanica, 'nothing burns in hell but the self'). Or else they can identify themselves with the inner man, in which case it becomes possible for them, as Suso shows, to ascend again, through unitive knowledge, to the Trinity and even, beyond the Trinity, to the ultimate Unity of the Divine Ground.

Within the Mohammedan tradition such a rationalization of the immediate mystical experience would have been dangerously unorthodox. Nevertheless, one has the impression, while reading certain Sufi texts, that their authors did in fact conceive of *al haqq*, the Real, as being the Divine Ground or Unity of Allah, underlying the active and personal aspects of the Godhead.

The second doctrine of the Perennial Philosophy —that it is possible to know the Divine Ground by a direct intuition higher than discursive reasoning— is to be found in all the great religions of the world. A philosopher who is content merely to know about the ultimate Reality—theoretically and by hearsay —is compared by Buddha to a herdsman of other men's cows. Mohammed uses an even homelier barnyard metaphor. For him the philosopher who has not realized his metaphysics is just an ass bearing a load of books. Christian, Hindu and Taoist teachers wrote no less emphatically about the absurd pretensions of mere learning and analytical reasoning. In the words of the Anglican Prayer Book, our eternal life, now and hereafter, 'stands in the knowledge of God'; and this knowledge is not discursive but 'of the heart,' a super-rational intuition, direct, synthetic and timeless.

The third doctrine of the Perennial Philosophy, that which affirms the double nature of man, is fundamental in all the higher religions. The unitive knowledge of the Divine Ground has, as its necessary condition, self-abnegation and charity. Only by means of self-abnegation and charity can we clear away the evil, folly and ignorance which constitute the thing we call our personality and prevent us from becoming aware of the spark of divinity illuminating the inner man. But the spark within is akin to the Divine Ground. By identifying ourselves with the first we can come to unitive knowledge of the second. These empirical facts of the spiritual life have been variously rationalized in terms of the theologies of the various religions. The

Hindus categorically affirm that thou art That—that
the indwelling Atman is the same as Brahman. For
orthodox Christianity there is not an identity between the spark and God. Union of the human
spirit with God takes place—union so complete
that the word 'deification' is applied to it; but it is
not the union of identical substances. According to
Christian theology, the saint is 'deified,' not because
Atman is Brahman, but because God has assimilated
the purified human spirit into the divine substance
by an act of grace. Islamic theology seems to make
a similar distinction. The Sufi, Mansur, was executed
for giving to the words 'union' and 'deification' the
literal meaning which they bear in the Hindu tradition. For our present purposes, however, the sig-
nificant fact is that these words are actually used by
Christians and Mohammedans to describe the empirical facts of metaphysical realization by means of
direct, super-rational intuition.

In regard to man's final end, all the higher religions are in complete agreement. The purpose of
human life is the discovery of Truth, the unitive
knowledge of the Godhead. The degree to which
this unitive knowledge is achieved here on earth
determines the degree to which it will be enjoyed
in the posthumous state. Contemplation of truth
is the end, action the means. In India, in China, in
ancient Greece, in Christian Europe, this was regarded as the most obvious and axiomatic piece
of orthodoxy. The invention of the steam engine
produced a revolution, not merely in industrial tech-
niques, but also and much more significantly in philosophy. Because machines could be made progres-
sively more and more efficient, western man came
to believe that men and societies would automatically register a corresponding moral and spiritual
improvement. Attention and allegiance came to be

paid, not to Eternity, but to the Utopian future. External circumstances came to be regarded as more important than states of mind about external circumstances, and the end of human life was held to be action, with contemplation as a means to that end. These false and, historically, aberrant and heretical doctrines are now systematically taught in our schools and repeated, day in, day out, by those anonymous writers of advertising copy who, more than any other teachers, provide European and American adults with their current philosophy of life. And so effective has been the propaganda that even professing Christians accept the heresy unquestioningly and are quite unconscious of its complete incompatibility with their own or anybody else's religion.

These four doctrines constitute the Perennial Philosophy in its minimal and basic form. A man who can practise what the Indians call Jnana yoga (the metaphysical discipline of discrimination between the Real and the apparent) asks for nothing more. This simple working hypothesis is enough for his purposes. But such discrimination is exceedingly difficult and can hardly be practised, at any rate in the preliminary stages of the spiritual life, except by persons endowed with a particular kind of mental constitution. That is why most statements of the Perennial Philosophy have included another doctrine, affirming the existence of one or more human Incarnations of the Divine Ground, by whose mediation and grace the worshipper is helped to achieve his goal—that unitive knowledge of the Godhead, which is man's eternal life and beatitude. The Bhagavad-Gita is one such statement. Here, Krishna is an Incarnation of the Divine Ground in human form. Similarly, in Christian and Buddhist theology, Jesus and Gotama are Incarnations of divinity. But where-

as in Hinduism and Buddhism more than one Incarnation of the Godhead is possible (and is regarded as having in fact taken place), for Christians
there has been and can be only one.

An Incarnation of the Godhead and, to a lesser
degree, any theocentric saint, sage or prophet is a
human being who knows Who he is and can therefore effectively remind other human beings of what
they have allowed themselves to forget: namely,
that if they choose to become what potentially they
already are, they too can be eternally united with
the Divine Ground.

Worship of the Incarnation and contemplation
of his attributes are for most men and women the
best preparation for unitive knowledge of the Godhead. But whether the actual knowledge itself can
be achieved by this means is another question. Many
Catholic mystics have affirmed that, at a certain
stage of that contemplative prayer in which, according to the most authoritative theologians, the life of
Christian perfection ultimately consists, it is necessary to put aside all thoughts of the Incarnation as
distracting from the higher knowledge of that which
has been incarnated. From this fact have arisen
misunderstandings in plenty and a number of intellectual difficulties. Here, for example, is what Abbot
John Chapman writes in one of his admirable Spiritual Letters: 'The problem of *reconciling* (not
merely uniting) mysticism with Christianity is more
difficult. The Abbot (Abbot Marmion) says that
St John of the Cross is like a sponge full of Christianity. You can squeeze it all out, and the full mystical theory remains. Consequently, for fifteen years
or so, I hated St John of the Cross and called him
a Buddhist. I loved St Teresa, and read her over
and over again. She is first a Christian, only second-
arily a mystic. Then I found that I had wasted

fifteen years, so far as prayer was concerned.' And yet, he concludes, in spite of its 'Buddhistic' character, the practice of mysticism (or, to put it in other terms, the realization of the Perennial Philosophy) makes good Christians. He might have added that it also makes good Hindus, good Buddhists, good Taoists, good Moslems and good Jews.

The solution to Abbot Chapman's problem must be sought in the domain, not of philosophy, but of psychology. Human beings are not born identical. There are many different temperaments and constitutions; and within each psycho-physical class one can find people at very different stages of spiritual development. Forms of worship and spiritual discipline which may be valuable for one individual may be useless or even positively harmful for another belonging to a different class and standing, within that class, at a lower or higher level of development. All this is clearly set forth in the Gita, where the psychological facts are linked up with general cosmology by means of the postulate of the *gunas*. Krishna, who is here the mouthpiece of Hinduism in all its manifestations, finds it perfectly natural that different men should have different methods and even apparently different objects of worship. All roads lead to Rome—provided, of course, that it is Rome and not some other city which the traveller really wishes to reach. A similar attitude of charitable inclusiveness, somewhat surprising in a Moslem, is beautifully expressed in the parable of Moses and the Shepherd, told by Jalaluddin Rumi in the second book of the Masnavi. And within the more exclusive Christian tradition these problems of temperament and degree of development have been searchingly discussed in their relation to the way of Mary and the way of Martha in general, and in particular to the vocation and private devotion of individuals.

We now have to consider the ethical corollaries of the Perennial Philosophy. 'Truth,' says St Thomas Aquinas, 'is the last end for the entire universe, and the contemplation of truth is the chief occupation of wisdom.' The moral virtues, he says in another place, belong to contemplation, not indeed essentially, but as a necessary predisposition. Virtue, in other words, is not the end, but the indispensable means to the knowledge of divine reality. Shankara, the greatest of the Indian commentators on the Gita, holds the same doctrine. Right action is the way to knowledge; for it purifies the mind, and it is only to a mind purified from egotism that the intuition of the Divine Ground can come.

Self-abnegation, according to the Gita, can be achieved by the practice of two all-inclusive virtues—love and non-attachment. The latter is the same thing as that 'holy indifference,' on which St François de Sales is never tired of insisting. 'He who refers every action to God,' writes Camus, summarizing his master's teaching, 'and has no aims save His Glory, will find rest everywhere, even amidst the most violent commotions.' So long as we practise this holy indifference to the fruits of action, 'no lawful occupation will separate us from God; on the contrary, it can be made a means of closer union.' Here the word 'lawful' supplies a necessary qualification to a teaching which, without it, is incomplete and even potentially dangerous. Some actions are intrinsically evil or inexpedient; and no good intentions, no conscious offering of them to God, no renunciation of the fruits can alter their essential character. Holy indifference requires to be taught in conjunction not merely with a set of commandments prohibiting crimes, but also with a clear conception of what in Buddha's Eightfold Path is called 'right livelihood.' Thus, for the Buddhist, right livelihood was incompatible with the making of deadly weapons and of intoxicants; for the mediæval Christian, with the taking of interest and with various monopolistic practices which have since come to be regarded as legitimate good business. John Woolman, the American Quaker, provides a most enlightening example of the way in which a man may live in the world, while practising perfect non-attachment and remaining acutely sensitive to the claims of right livelihood. Thus, while it would have been profitable and perfectly lawful for him to sell West Indian sugar and rum to the customers who came to his shop, Woolman refrained from doing so, because these things were the products of slave labour. Similarly, when he was in England, it would have been both lawful and convenient for him to travel by stage coach. Nevertheless, he preferred to make his journeys on foot. Why? Because the comforts of rapid travel could only be brought at the expense of great cruelty to the horses and the most atrocious working conditions for the post-boys. In Woolman's eyes, such a system of transportation was intrinsically undesirable, and no amount of personal non-attachment could make it anything but undesirable. So he shouldered his knapsack and walked.

In the preceding pages I have tried to show that the Perennial Philosophy and its ethical corollaries constitute a Highest Common Factor, present in all the major religions of the world. To affirm this truth has never been more imperatively necessary than at the present time. There will never be enduring peace unless and until human beings come to accept a philosophy of life more adequate to the cosmic and psychological facts than the insane idolatries of nationalism and the advertising man's apocalyptic faith in Progress towards a mechanized New Jerusalem. All the elements of this philosophy are present, as we have seen, in the traditional religions. But in existing circumstances there is not the slightest chance that any of the traditional religions will obtain universal acceptance. Europeans and Americans will see no reason for being converted to Hinduism, say, or Buddhism. And the people of Asia can hardly be expected to renounce their own traditions for the Christianity professed, often sincerely, by the imperialists who, for four hundred years and more, have been systematically attacking, exploiting and oppressing, and are now trying to finish off the work of destruction by 'educating' them. But happily there is the Highest Common Factor of all religions, the Perennial Philosophy which has always and everywhere been the metaphysical system of the prophets, saints and sages. It is perfectly possible for people to remain good Christians, Hindus, Buddhists or Moslems and yet to be united in full agreement on the basic doctrines of the Perennial Philosophy.

The Bhagavad-Gita is perhaps the most systematic scriptural statement of the Perennial Philosophy. To a world at war, a world that, because it lacks the intellectual and spiritual prerequisites to peace, can only hope to patch up some kind of precarious armed truce, it stands pointing, clearly and unmistakably, to the only road of escape from the self-imposed necessity of self-destruction. For this reason we should be grateful to Swami Prabhavananda and Mr Isherwood for having given us this new version of the book—a version which can be read, not merely without that dull æsthetic pain inflicted by all too many English translations from the Sanskrit, but positively with enjoyment.

ALDOUS HUXLEY

Gita and Mahabharata

THE MAHABHARATA is said to be the longest poem in the world. In its original form, it consisted of twenty-four thousand verses, and it grew to about one hundred thousand. Like the Old Testament, it is not a homogeneous work, but a collection of narratives. Its central theme, as the name indicates, is the story of the descendants of King Bharata (*Maha* means great), and of ancient India, the land where the Bharatas lived and ruled.

After the death of King Pandu, the Mahabharata tells us, his brother Dhritarashtra succeeded to the throne. Dhritarashtra educated the five sons of Pandu, the Pandavas, along with his own one hundred sons. As they grew to be men, the Pandavas distinguished themselves by their piety and heroic virtues. In consequence, Duryodhana, Dhritarashtra's eldest son, became jealous and planned to murder them.

Duryodhana's scheme was to build a palace in a distant town, and invite the Pandavas to stay there during a religious festival. The palace was made of specially inflammable materials, so that Duryodhana's servants could easily set it on fire. It burned to ashes, but the Pandavas and Kunti, their mother, had been warned in time, and escaped. Duryodhana believed them dead.

The Pandavas lived in the forest, disguised as Brahmins, meeting all kinds of dangers and adventures. One day they heard that a neighbouring king was to choose a husband for his daughter. The winner must bend a bow of enormous strength and hit a tiny target. The Pandavas thought they would try. They went to the city in their disguise.

Suitors had gathered from all over India, Duryo-

dhana among them. One after another, they failed in
the test. At last Arjuna, third of the Pandavas, stood
up, bent the bow and hit the target with the greatest
ease. Draupadi, the princess, threw him the victor's
garland. But the assembled princes could not accept
this humiliation at the hands of a seemingly poor
and unwarlike Brahmin. There would have been a
fight—just as in the story of Ulysses—if Krishna, who
was present, had not intervened and persuaded
them that Arjuna had a right to his bride. Krishna
was a cousin of the Pandavas, but he was not one of
Dhritarashtra's sons.

The brothers took Draupadi back to the forest,
where Kunti was awaiting them. 'Mother,' they
cried, 'we have brought home a wonderful treasure!'
'Be sure to share it equally, my children,' Kunti
answered; then she saw the girl, and exclaimed in
dismay: 'Oh, what have I said!' But it was too late.
Her word was sacred to her sons. So Draupadi mar-
ried all the brothers together.

Dhritarashtra and his son now knew that the Pandavas were not only alive, but allied by marriage to
a powerful monarch. Duryodhana was for carrying
on the feud, but Dhritarashtra wisely listened to
the advice of his uncle Bhisma, which was to send
for the brothers and offer them half of his kingdom.
So the kingdom was divided. The Pandavas got the
worst of the land, a wilderness along the Jamuna
River. They cleared it, built a fine city, and crowned
Yudhisthira, the eldest brother, as their king.

Now the five brothers lived in triumph and splendour, and Duryodhana hated them more than ever.
His jealousy hatched a new plot for their ruin. The
pious and noble Yudhisthira had a dangerous weakness for gambling. So Duryodhana challenged him to
play dice with a clever sharper named Sakuni, knowing that the king would feel bound in honour to

accept. They played, Sakuni cheated, Yudhisthira lost game after game, staking his wealth, his kingdom, and finally his brothers, Draupadi and himself. All were now the slaves of Duryodhana's vengeance, subject to insult and cruelty, until Dhritarashtra intervened, and insisted that they be set at liberty and their kingdom given back.

But Duryodhana worked upon his father until he obtained permission for another dice-match. The loser was to forfeit his kingdom and retire to the forest for twelve years, then he must live for a year in the city without being recognized; if he was discovered, the term of exile would begin again. This game Yudhisthira also lost. So the Pandavas went back to the forest. They made a virtue of their misfortune, practising spiritual austerities and doing many heroic deeds.

Once, during their wanderings, we are told, the brothers suffered greatly from thirst. Nakula, the youngest, was sent to look for water. He found a lake which was clear as crystal. As he bent over it, a voice said: 'Stop, child. First answer my questions. Then you may drink.' But Nakula, in his desperate thirst, paid no attention to the voice: he drank, and immediately fell dead. His brother Sahadeva went out to look for him. He, too, found the lake, and the same thing happened. In this manner, four of the brothers died.

Last of all came Yudhisthira. He found the corpses, and began to lament. Then the voice told him: 'Child, first answer my questions, and then I will cure your grief and your thirst.' He turned, and saw Dharma, the personification of duty and virtue, standing beside him in the form of a crane.

'What is the road to heaven?' the crane asked.

'Truthfulness.'

'How does a man find happiness?'

'Through right conduct.'

'What must he subdue, in order to escape grief?'

'His mind.'

'When is a man loved?'

'When he is without vanity.'

'Of all the world's wonders, which is the most wonderful?'

'That no man, though he sees others dying all around him, believes that he himself will die.'

'How does one reach true religion?'

'Not by argument. Not by scriptures and doctrines; they cannot help. The path to religion is trodden by the saints.'

Dharma was satisfied. He revealed himself to Yudhisthira. Then he brought the four brothers back to life.

When the period of exile was over at last, Yudhisthira asked for the return of his kingdom; but Duryodhana refused. Yudhisthira said he would be content with just one village for himself and for each of his brothers. But Duryodhana, in the insanity of his greed, would not agree even to this. The older members of the family tried to arbitrate, and failed. So war became inevitable. Neighbouring kings were drawn into the quarrel, until the whole of India was involved. Both sides wanted Krishna's aid. To both, Krishna offered the same choice. 'Either you can have the help of my kinsmen, the Vrishnis, in the battle,' he told them, 'or you can have me alone. But I shall take no part in the fighting.' Duryodhana chose the Vrishnis. Arjuna preferred to take Krishna himself, as his personal charioteer.

The battle was fought on the plain of Kurukshetra, a sacred place of pilgrimage. It was here, just before the armies engaged, that Krishna and Arjuna had the conversation which is recorded in the Bhagavad-Gita.

The battle lasted eighteen days, and ended with the death of Duryodhana and the complete victory of the Pandavas. Thereafter, Yudhisthira became undisputed ruler of India. He reigned for thirty-six years.

The story ends with the pilgrimage of Draupadi and the Pandavas up the heights of the Himalayas to the abode of God. On the way, the queen and four of the brothers died: they were not sufficiently pure to be able to enter heaven in their human bodies. Only Yudhisthira, the royal saint, journeyed on, accompanied by his faithful dog. When they reached heaven, Indra, the king of gods, told him that the dog could not come in. Yudhisthira replied that, if this was so, he would stay outside heaven too; for he could not bring himself to desert any creature which trusted him and wished for his protection. Finally, after a long argument, both dog and king were admitted. Then the dog was revealed as Dharma himself. This had been another test of Yudhisthira's spiritual greatness. One more was to follow. When the king looked around him, he found that heaven was filled with his mortal enemies. Where, he asked, were his brothers and his comrades? Indra conducted him to a gloomy and horrible region, the pit of hell itself. 'I prefer to stay here,' said Yudhisthira, 'for the place where they are is heaven to me.' At this, the blackness and horror vanished. Yudhisthira and the other Pandavas passed beyond the appearance of hell and heaven into the true Being of God which is immortality.

The Bhagavad-Gita (meaning, literally, the Song of God) is not regarded by Hindus as Sruti (scriptural teaching actually revealed by God to man, as in the Upanishads) but only as Smriti (the teaching of divine incarnations, saints or prophets, who fur-

their explain and eloborate the God-given truths of
the scriptures). Nevertheless, it is the most popular
book in Hindu religious literature; the Gospel, one
may say, of India. It has profoundly influenced the
spiritual, cultural, intellectual and political life of
the country throughout the centuries, and it con-
tinues to do so to-day. Every westerner should study
it if he wants to understand the mental processes of
India's thinkers and leaders.

The date of the Gita is generally placed by scholars somewhere between the fifth and second centuries, B.C. Most of them agree that it was not orig-
inally a part of the Mahabharata itself, but this does
not necessarily mean that it was composed later
than the epic. It seems to have existed for some time
independently.

In the Gita dialogue there are four speakers: King
Dhritarashtra, Sanjaya, Arjuna and Krishna.

Dhritarashtra is blind. The sage Vyasa (who is
traditionally supposed to be the author of the Gita)
offers to restore his sight, in order that he may
watch the battle of Kurukshetra. But Dhritarashtra
refuses. He cannot bear to see his kinsmen killed.
So Vyasa confers the psychic powers of clairvoyance
and clairaudience upon Sanjaya, who is Dhritarashtra's minister and charioteer. As they sit together
in the palace, Sanjaya describes to his master everything he sees and hears on the distant battlefield.
Through his mouth, the words of Krishna and Arjuna are mediumistically reported. Occasionally, he
pauses in his report to add descriptive remarks of
his own.

Sri Krishna (*Sri* is a title of reverence, such as
Lord) has been called the Christ of India. There are,
in fact, some striking parallels between the life of
Krishna, as related in the Bhagavatam and elsewhere, and the life of Jesus of Nazareth. In both

cases, legend and fact mingle; but the historical problem has nothing to do with a consideration of the message of the Bhagavad-Gita. To a seeker after spiritual reality who reads the Gita or the Sermon on the Mount, it cannot matter very much whether or not the historical Krishna and the historical Jesus ever existed at all.

The Gita is not primarily concerned with Krishna as an individual, but with his aspect as Brahman, the ultimate Reality. When Krishna addresses Arjuna, he sometimes speaks as an individual, but often as God Himself:

> For I am Brahman
> Within this body,
> Life immortal
> That shall not perish:
> I am the Truth
> And the Joy forever.

Arjuna, in his attitude to Krishna, also expresses this dual relationship. Krishna is the divine incarnation of Vishnu, Arjuna's chosen deity. Arjuna knows this—yet, by a merciful ignorance, he sometimes forgets. Indeed, it is Krishna who makes him forget, since no ordinary man could bear the strain of constant companionship with God. After the vision of Krishna's divine aspect, which is recorded in chapter eleven, Arjuna is appalled by the realization that he has been treating the Lord of the universe as 'friend and fellow-mortal.' He humbly begs Krishna's pardon, but his awe soon leaves him. Again, he has forgotten. We may infer the same relationship between Jesus and his disciples after the vision of the transfiguration.

King Dhritarashtra speaks but once. In fact, the whole narrative of the Gita is Sanjaya's answer to his single opening question.

I. The Sorrow of Arjuna*

DHRITARASHTRA:

Tell me, Sanjaya, what my sons and the sons of Pandu did, when they gathered on the sacred field of Kurukshetra eager for battle?

(In the following verses, Sanjaya describes how Duryodhana, seeing the opposing army of Pandavas in array, went to Drona, his teacher, and expressed his fear that their own army was the weaker of the two, although numerically larger. He named the leading warriors on either side. This is one of the catalogue-passages to be found in nearly all epics. It need not be translated in full.

In order to raise Duryodhana's failing courage, Bhisma, the commander-in-chief, sounded his conch-shell horn. But this was ill-advised—for the enemy chieftains immediately blew their horns in reply, and made much more noise. The trumpeting 'resounded through heaven and earth,' we are told.

Arjuna now addresses Krishna, his friend and charioteer.)

ARJUNA:

Krishna the changeless,
Halt my chariot
There where the warriors,
Bold for the battle,
Face their foemen.
Between the armies
There let me see them,
The men I must fight with,
Gathered together
Now at the bidding

* The accent is on the first syllable.

Of him their leader,
Blind Dhritarashtra's
Evil offspring:
Such are my foes
In the war that is coming.

SANJAYA (TO DHRITARASHTRA):

Then Krishna, subduer of the senses, thus requested by Arjuna, the conqueror of sloth,* drove that most splendid of chariots into a place between the two armies, confronting Bhisma, Drona and all those other rulers of the earth. And he said: 'O Prince, behold the assembled Kurus!'

Then the prince looked on the array, and in both armies he recognized fathers and grandfathers, teachers, uncles, sons, brothers, grandsons, fathers-in-law, dear friends, and many other familiar faces.

When Kunti's son saw all those ranks of kinsmen he was filled with deep compassion, and he spoke despairingly, as follows:

ARJUNA:

Krishna, Krishna,
Now as I look on
These my kinsmen
Arrayed for battle,
My limbs are weakened,
My mouth is parching,
My body trembles,
My hair stands upright,
My skin seems burning,
The bow Gandiva
Slips from my hand,
My brain is whirling
Round and round,
I can stand no longer:
Krishna, I see such

---

* Arjuna is traditionally supposed to have lived entirely without sleep. We may take this to mean that he had overcome all forms of laziness.

Omens of evil!
What can we hope from
This killing of kinsmen?
What do I want with
Victory, empire,
Or their enjoyment?
O Govinda,*
How can I care for
Power or pleasure,
My own life, even,
When all these others,
Teachers, fathers,
Grandfathers, uncles,
Sons and brothers,
Husbands of sisters,
Grandsons and cousins,
For whose sake only
I could enjoy them
Stand here ready
To risk blood and wealth
In war against us?

Knower of all things,
Though they should slay me
How could I harm them?
I cannot wish it:
Never, never,
Not though it won me
The throne of the three worlds;
How much the less for
Earthly lordship!

Krishna, hearing
The prayers of all men,
Tell me how can
We hope to be happy
Slaying the sons

* One of the names of Sri Krishna, meaning Giver of Enlightenment.

Of Dhritarashtra?
Evil they may be,
Worst of the wicked,
Yet if we kill them
Our sin is greater.
How could we dare spill
The blood that unites us?
Where is joy in
The killing of kinsmen?

Foul their hearts are
With greed, and blinded:
They see no evil
In breaking of blood-bonds,
See no sin
In treason to comrades.
But we, clear-sighted,
Scanning the ruin
Of families scattered,
Should we not shun
This crime, O Krishna?

We know what fate falls
On families broken:
The rites are forgotten,
Vice rots the remnant
Defiling the women,
And from their corruption
Comes mixing of castes:
The curse of confusion
Degrades the victims
And damns the destroyers.
The rice and the water
No longer are offered;
The ancestors also
Must fall dishonoured
From home in heaven.

Such is the crime
Of the killers of kinsmen:
The ancient, the sacred,
Is broken, forgotten.
Such is the doom
Of the lost, without caste-rites:
Darkness and doubting
And hell for ever.

What is this crime
I am planning, O Krishna?
Murder most hateful,
Murder of brothers!
Am I indeed
So greedy for greatness?

Rather than this
Let the evil children
Of Dhritarashtra
Come with their weapons
Against me in battle:
I shall not struggle,
I shall not strike them.
Now let them kill me,
That will be better.

SANJAYA:

Having spoken thus, Arjuna threw aside his arrows
and his bow in the midst of the battlefield. He sat
down on the seat of the chariot, and his heart was
overcome with sorrow.

II. The Yoga of Knowledge

SANJAYA:

Then his eyes filled with tears, and his heart grieved and was bewildered with pity. And Sri Krishna spoke to him, saying:

SRI KRISHNA:

Arjuna, is this hour of battle the time for scruples and fancies? Are they worthy of you, who seek enlightenment? Any brave man who merely hopes for fame or heaven would despise them.

What is this weakness? It is beneath you. Is it for nothing men call you the foe-consumer? Shake off this cowardice, Arjuna. Stand up.

ARJUNA:

Bhisma and Drona are noble and ancient, worthy of the deepest reverence. How can I greet them with arrows, in battle? If I kill them, how can I ever enjoy my wealth, or any other pleasure? It will be cursed with blood-guilt. I would much rather spare them, and eat the bread of a beggar.

Which will be worse, to win this war, or to lose it? I scarcely know. Even the sons of Dhritarashtra stand in the enemy ranks. If we kill them, none of us will wish to live.

Is this real compassion that I feel, or only a delusion? My mind gropes about in darkness. I cannot see where my duty lies. Krishna, I beg you, tell me frankly and clearly what I ought to do. I am your disciple. I put myself into your hands. Show me the way.

Not this world's kingdom,
Supreme, unchallenged,
No, nor the throne

Of the gods in heaven,
Could ease this sorrow
That numbs my senses!

SANJAYA:

When Arjuna, the foe-consuming, the never-slothful, had spoken thus to Govinda, ruler of the senses, he added: 'I will not fight,' and was silent.

Then to him who thus sorrowed between the two armies, the ruler of the senses spoke, smiling:

SRI KRISHNA:

Your words are wise, Arjuna, but your sorrow is for nothing. The truly wise mourn neither for the living nor for the dead.

There was never a time when I did not exist, nor you, nor any of these kings. Nor is there any future in which we shall cease to be.

Just as the dweller in this body passes through childhood, youth and old age, so at death he merely passes into another kind of body. The wise are not deceived by that.

Feelings of heat and cold, pleasure and pain, are caused by the contact of the senses with their objects. They come and they go, never lasting long. You must accept them.

A serene spirit accepts pleasure and pain with an even mind, and is unmoved by either. He alone is worthy of immortality.

That which is non-existent can never come into being, and that which is can never cease to be. Those who have known the inmost Reality know also the nature of *is* and *is not*.

That Reality which pervades the universe is indestructible. No one has power to change the Changeless.

Bodies are said to die, but That which possesses the body is eternal. It cannot be limited, or destroyed. Therefore you must fight.

Some say this Atman*
Is slain, and others
Call It the slayer:
They know nothing.
How can It slay
Or who shall slay It?

Know this Atman
Unborn, undying,
Never ceasing,
Never beginning,
Deathless, birthless,
Unchanging for ever.
How can It die
The death of the body?

Knowing It birthless,
Knowing It deathless,
Knowing It endless,
For ever unchanging,
Dream not you do
The deed of the killer,
Dream not the power
Is yours to command it.

Worn-out garments
Are shed by the body:
Worn-out bodies
Are shed by the dweller
Within the body.
New bodies are donned
By the dweller, like garments.

Not wounded by weapons,
Not burned by fire,
Not dried by the wind,
Not wetted by water:
Such is the Atman,

* The Godhead that is within every being.

Not dried, not wetted,
Not burned, not wounded,
Innermost element,
Everywhere, always,
Being of beings,
Changeless, eternal,
For ever and ever.

This Atman cannot be manifested to the senses,
or thought about by the mind. It is not subject to
modification. Since you know this, you should not
grieve.

But if you should suppose this Atman to be subject to constant birth and death, even then you
ought not to be sorry.

Death is certain for the born. Rebirth is certain
for the dead. You should not grieve for what is un-
avoidable.

Before birth, beings are not manifest to our human senses. In the interim between birth and death,
they are manifest. At death they return to the unmanifest again. What is there in all this to grieve
over?

There are some who have actually looked upon
the Atman, and understood It, in all Its wonder.
Others can only speak of It as wonderful beyond
their understanding. Others know of Its wonder by
hearsay. And there are others who are told about
It and do not understand a word.

He Who dwells within all living bodies remains
for ever indestructible. Therefore, you should never
mourn for any one.

Even if you consider this from the standpoint of
your own caste-duty, you ought not to hesitate; for,
to a warrior, there is nothing nobler than a righteous
war. Happy are the warriors to whom a battle such
as this comes: it opens a door to heaven.

But if you refuse to fight this righteous war, you will be turning aside from your duty. You will be a sinner, and disgraced. People will speak ill of you throughout the ages. To a man who values his honour, that is surely worse than death. The warrior-chiefs will believe it was fear that drove you from the battle; you will be despised by those who have admired you so long. Your enemies, also, will slander your courage. They will use the words which should never be spoken. What could be harder to bear than that?

Die, and you win heaven. Conquer, and you enjoy the earth. Stand up now, son of Kunti, and resolve to fight. Realize that pleasure and pain, gain and loss, victory and defeat, are all one and the same: then go into battle. Do this and you cannot commit any sin.

I have explained to you the true nature of the Atman. Now listen to the method of Karma Yoga.* If you can understand and follow it, you will be able to break the chains of desire which bind you to your actions.

In this yoga, even the abortive attempt is not wasted. Nor can it produce a contrary result. Even a little practise of this yoga will save you from the terrible wheel of rebirth and death.

In this yoga, the will is directed singly toward one ideal. When a man lacks this discrimination, his will wanders in all directions, after innumerable aims.

* Karma: (1) Work, a deed.
    (2) Effect of a deed.
    (3) Law of causation governing action and its effects in the physical and psychological plane.

Yoga: (1) Union with God.
    (2) A prescribed path of spiritual life. The various yogas are, therefore, different paths to union with God. Karma Yoga is the path of selfless, God-dedicated action.

Yogi: One who practises yoga.

Those who lack discrimination may quote the letter
of the scripture, but they are really denying its inner
truth. They are full of worldly desires, and hungry
for the rewards of heaven. They use beautiful figures
of speech. They teach elaborate rituals which are
supposed to obtain pleasure and power for those
who perform them. But, actually, they understand
nothing except the law of Karma, that chains men
to rebirth.

Those whose discrimination is stolen away by
such talk grow deeply attached to pleasure and
power. And so they are unable to develop that concentration of the will which leads a man to absorption in God.

The Vedas[1] teach us about the three gunas[2] and
their functions. You, Arjuna, must overcome the
three gunas. You must be free from the pairs of
opposites.[3] Poise your mind in tranquillity. Take care
neither to acquire nor to hoard. Be established in
the consciousness of the Atman, always.

When the whole country is flooded, the reservoir
becomes superfluous. So, to the illumined seer, the
Vedas are all superfluous.

You have the right to work, but for the work's
sake only. You have no right to the fruits of work.
Desire for the fruits of work must never be your
motive in working. Never give way to laziness,
either.

Perform every action with your heart fixed on the
Supreme Lord. Renounce attachment to the fruits.
Be even-tempered in success and failure; for it is
this evenness of temper which is meant by yoga.

[1] Revealed scriptures of the Hindus. The reference here is to the ritualistic
portion of the Vedas.

[2] The three forces or substances composing the universe of mind and matter.
They are sattwa, rajas and tamas.

[3] Heat and cold, pleasure and pain, etc. The seeming contradictions of the relative
world.

Work done with anxiety about results is far inferior to work done without such anxiety, in the calm of self-surrender. Seek refuge in the knowledge of Brahman.* They who work selfishly for results are miserable.

In the calm of self-surrender you can free yourself from the bondage of virtue and vice during this very life. Devote yourself, therefore, to reaching union with Brahman. To unite the heart with Brahman and then to act: that is the secret of non-attached work. In the calm of self-surrender, the seers renounce the fruits of their actions, and so reach enlightenment. Then they are free from the bondage of rebirth, and pass to that state which is beyond all evil.

When your intellect has cleared itself of its delusions, you will become indifferent to the results of all action, present or future. At present, your intellect is bewildered by conflicting interpretations of the scriptures. When it can rest, steady and undistracted, in contemplation of the Atman, then you will reach union with the Atman.

ARJUNA:

Krishna, how can one identify a man who is firmly established and absorbed in Brahman? In what manner does an illumined soul speak? How does he sit? How does he walk?

SRI KRISHNA:

He knows bliss in the Atman
And wants nothing else.
Cravings torment the heart:
He renounces cravings.
I call him illumined.

* The Godhead.

Not shaken by adversity,
Not hankering after happiness:
Free from fear, free from anger,
Free from the things of desire.
1 call him a seer, and illumined.
The bonds of his flesh are broken.
He is lucky, and does not rejoice:
He is unlucky, and does not weep.
I call him illumined.

The tortoise can draw in his legs:
The seer can draw in his senses.
I call him illumined.

The abstinent run away from what they desire
But carry their desires with them:
When a man enters Reality,
He leaves his desires behind him.

Even a mind that knows the path
Can be dragged from the path:
The senses are so unruly.
But he controls the senses
And recollects the mind
And fixes it on me.
I call him illumined.

Thinking about sense-objects
Will attach you to sense-objects;
Grow attached, and you become addicted;
Thwart your addiction, it turns to anger;
Be angry, and you confuse your mind;
Confuse your mind, you forget the lesson of experi-
    ence;
Forget experience, you lose discrimination;
Lose discrimination, and you miss life's only pur-
    pose.

When he has no lust, no hatred,
A man walks safely among the things of lust and
    hatred.
To obey the Atman
Is his peaceful joy:
Sorrow melts
Into that clear peace:
His quiet mind
Is soon established in peace.

The uncontrolled mind
Does not guess that the Atman is present:
How can it meditate?
Without meditation, where is peace?
Without peace, where is happiness?

The wind turns a ship
From its course upon the waters:
The wandering winds of the senses
Cast man's mind adrift
And turn his better judgment from its course.
When a man can still the senses
I call him illumined.
The recollected mind is awake
In the knowledge of the Atman
Which is dark night to the ignorant:
The ignorant are awake in their sense-life
Which they think is daylight:
To the seer it is darkness.

Water flows continually into the ocean
But the ocean is never disturbed:
Desire flows into the mind of the seer
But he is never disturbed.
The seer knows peace:
The man who stirs up his own lusts

Can never know peace.
He knows peace who has forgotten desire.
He lives without craving:
Free from ego, free from pride.

This is the state of enlightenment in Brahman:
A man does not fall back from it
Into delusion.
Even at the moment of death
He is alive in that enlightenment:
Brahman and he are one.

III. Karma Yoga

ARJUNA:

But, Krishna, if you consider knowledge of Brahman superior to any sort of action, why are you telling me to do these terrible deeds?

Your statements seem to contradict each other. They confuse my mind. Tell me one definite way of reaching the highest good.

SRI KRISHNA:

I have already told you that, in this world, aspirants may find enlightenment by two different paths. For the contemplative is the path of knowledge: for the active is the path of selfless action.

Freedom from activity is never achieved by abstaining from action. Nobody can become perfect by merely ceasing to act. In fact, nobody can ever rest from his activity* even for a moment. All are helplessly forced to act, by the gunas.

A man who renounces certain physical actions but still lets his mind dwell on the objects of his sensual

* Here 'activity' includes mental action, conscious and sub-conscious.

desire, is deceiving himself. He can only be called a hypocrite. The truly admirable man controls his senses by the power of his will. All his actions are disinterested. All are directed along the path to union with Brahman.

Activity is better than inertia. Act, but with self-control. If you are lazy, you cannot even sustain your own body.

The world is imprisoned in its own activity, except when actions are performed as worship of God. Therefore you must perform every action sacramentally, and be free from all attachments to results.

> In the beginning
> The Lord of beings
> Created all men,
> To each his duty.
> 'Do this,' He said,
> 'And you shall prosper.
> Duty well done
> Fulfils desire
> Like Kamadhenu[1]
> The wish-fulfiller.'
> 'Doing of duty
> Honours the devas:[2]
> To you the devas
> In turn will be gracious:
> Each honouring other,
> Man reaches the Highest.
> Please the devas:
> Your prayer will be granted.'
> But he who enjoys the devas' bounty
> Showing no thanks,
> He thieves from the devas.

[1] A legendary cow, mentioned in the Mahabharata.
[2] The inhabitants of heaven.

Pious men eat
What the gods leave over
After the offering:
Thus they are sinless.
But those ungodly
Cooking good food
For the greed of their stomachs
Sin as they eat it.
Food quickens the life-sperm:
Food grows from the rainfall
Called down out of heaven
By sacrifice offered:
Sacrifice speaks
Through the act of the ritual.
This is the ritual
Taught by the sacred
Scriptures that spring
From the lips of the Changeless:
Know therefore that Brahman
The all-pervading
Is dwelling for ever
Within this ritual.

If a man plays no part
In the acts thus appointed
His living is evil
His joy is in lusting.
Know this, O Prince:
His life is for nothing.

But when a man has found delight and satisfaction and peace in the Atman, then he is no longer obliged to perform any kind of action. He has nothing to gain in this world by action, and nothing to lose by refraining from action. He is independent of everybody and everything. Do your duty, always; but without attachment. That is how a man reaches the ultimate Truth; by working without anxiety about results. In fact, Janaka* and many others reached enlightenment, simply because they did their duty in this spirit. Your motive in working should be to set others, by your example, on the path of duty.

Whatever a great man does, ordinary people will imitate; they follow his example. Consider me: I am not bound by any sort of duty. There is nothing, in all the three worlds, which I do not already possess; nothing I have yet to acquire. But I go on working, nevertheless. If I did not continue to work untiringly as I do, mankind would still follow me, no matter where I led them. Suppose I were to stop? They would all be lost. The result would be caste-mixture and universal destruction.

> The ignorant work
> For the fruit of their action:
> The wise must work also
> Without desire
> Pointing man's feet
> To the path of his duty.
>
> Let the wise beware
> Lest they bewilder
> The minds of the ignorant
> Hungry for action:
> Let them show by example
> How work is holy
> When the heart of the worker
> Is fixed on the Highest.

Every action is really performed by the gunas. Man, deluded by his egoism, thinks: 'I am the doer.' But he who has the true insight into the operations of the gunas and their various functions, knows that

* A royal saint mentioned in the Upanishads.

when senses attach themselves to objects, gunas are merely attaching themselves to gunas. Knowing this, he does not become attached to his actions.

The illumined soul must not create confusion in the minds of the ignorant by refraining from work. The ignorant, in their delusion, identify the Atman with the gunas. They become tied to the senses and the action of the senses.

Shake off this fever of ignorance. Stop hoping for worldly rewards. Fix your mind on the Atman. Be free from the sense of ego. Dedicate all your actions to me. Then go forward and fight.

If a man keeps following my teaching with faith in his heart, and does not make mental reservations, he will be released from the bondage of his karma. But those who scorn my teaching, and do not follow it, are lost. They are without spiritual discrimination. All their knowledge is a delusion.

Even a wise man acts according to the tendencies of his own nature. All living creatures follow their tendencies. What use is any external restraint? The attraction and aversion which the senses feel for different objects are natural. But you must not give way to such feelings; they are obstacles.

It is better to do your own duty, however imperfectly, than to assume the duties of another person, however successfully. Prefer to die doing your own duty: the duty of another will bring you into great spiritual danger.

ARJUNA:

Krishna, what is it that makes a man do evil, even against his own will; under compulsion, as it were?

SRI KRISHNA:

The rajo-guna has two faces,
Rage and lust: the ravenous, the deadly:
Recognize these: they are your enemies.

Smoke hides fire,
Dust hides a mirror,
The womb hides the embryo:
By lust the Atman is hidden.

Lust hides the Atman in its hungry flames,
The wise man's faithful foe.
Intellect, senses and mind
Are fuel to its fire:
Thus it deludes
The dweller in the body,
Bewildering his judgment.

Therefore, Arjuna, you must first control your senses, then kill this evil thing which obstructs discriminative knowledge and realization of the Atman.

The senses are said to be higher than the sense-objects. The mind is higher than the senses. The intelligent will is higher than the mind. What is higher than the intelligent will? The Atman Itself.

You must know Him who is above the intelligent will. Get control of the mind through spiritual discrimination. Then destroy your elusive enemy, who wears the form of lust.

IV. Renunciation Through Knowledge

SRI KRISHNA:
Foe-consumer,
Now I have shown you
Yoga that leads
To the truth undying.
I taught this yoga
First to Vivaswat,

Vivaswat taught it
In turn to Manu,
Next Ikshaku
Learnt it from Manu,
And so the sages
In royal succession
Carried it onward
From teacher to teacher,
Till at length it was lost,
Throughout ages forgotten.

ARJUNA:

Vivaswat was born long before you. How am I to
believe that you were the first to teach this yoga?

SRI KRISHNA:

You and I, Arjuna,
Have lived many lives.
I remember them all:
You do not remember.

I am the birthless, the deathless,
Lord of all that breathes.
I seem to be born:
It is only seeming,
Only my Maya.*
I am still master
Of my Prakriti,*
The power that makes me.

When goodness grows weak,
When evil increases,
I make myself a body.

In every age I come back
To deliver the holy,
To destroy the sin of the sinner,
To establish righteousness.

* The two words are interchangeable. They both refer to the creative power of
Brahman, and, hence, to the basic stuff of which the universe is made.

He who knows the nature
Of my task and my holy birth
Is not reborn
When he leaves this body:
He comes to me.

Flying from fear,
From lust and anger,
He hides in me
His refuge, his safety:
Burnt clean in the blaze of my being,
In me many find home.

Whatever wish men bring me in worship,
That wish I grant them.
Whatever path men travel
Is my path:
No matter where they walk
It leads to me.

Most men worship the gods because they want success in their worldly undertakings. This kind of material success can be gained very quickly, here on earth.

I established the four castes, which correspond to the different types of guna and karma. I am their author; nevertheless, you must realize that I am beyond action and changeless. Action does not contaminate me. I have no desire at all for the fruits of action. A man who understands my nature in this respect will never become the slave of his own activity. Because they understood this, the ancient seekers for liberation could safely engage in action. You, too, must do your work in the spirit of those early seers.

What is action? What is inaction? Even the wise are puzzled by this question. Therefore, I will tell

you what action is. When you know that, you will
be free from all impurity. You must learn what kind
of work to do, what kind of work to avoid, and how
to reach a state of calm detachment from your work.
The real nature of action is hard to understand.

He who sees the inaction that is in action, and the
action that is in inaction, is wise indeed. Even when
he is engaged in action he remains poised in the
tranquillity of the Atman.

> The seers say truly
> That he is wise
> Who acts without lust or scheming
> For the fruit of the act:
> His act falls from him,
> Its chain is broken,
> Melted in the flame of my knowledge.
> Turning his face from the fruit,
> He needs nothing:
> The Atman is enough.
> He acts, and is beyond action.
>
> Not hoping, not lusting,
> Bridling body and mind,
> He calls nothing his own:
> He acts, and earns no evil.
>
> What God's Will gives
> He takes, and is contented.
> Pain follows pleasure,
> He is not troubled:
> Gain follows loss,
> He is indifferent:
> Of whom should he be jealous?
> He acts, and is not bound by his action.

When the bonds are broken
His illumined heart
Beats in Brahman:
His every action
Is worship of Brahman:
Can such acts bring evil?
Brahman is the ritual,
Brahman is the offering,
Brahman is he who offers
To the fire that is Brahman.
If a man sees Brahman
In every action,
He will find Brahman.*

Some yogis merely worship the devas. Others are able, by the grace of the Atman, to meditate on the identity of the Atman with Brahman. For these, the Atman is the offering, and Brahman the sacrificial fire into which It is offered.

Some withdraw all their senses from contact with exterior sense-objects. For these, hearing and other senses are the offering, and self-discipline the sacrificial fire. Others allow their minds and senses to wander unchecked, and try to see Brahman within all exterior sense-objects. For these, sound and the other sense-objects are the offering, and sense-enjoyment the sacrificial fire.

Some renounce all the actions of the senses, and all the functions of the vital force. For these, such actions and functions are the offering, and the practice of self-control is the sacrificial fire, kindled by knowledge of the Atman.

Then there are others whose way of worship is to renounce sense-objects and material possessions. Others set themselves austerities and spiritual dis-

* This verse is chanted by all Hindu monks as a grace before meals. In this case 'the fire' is regarded as the fire of hunger.

ciplines: that is their way of worship. Others worship through the practice of Raja Yoga.* Others who are earnest seekers for perfection and men of strict vows, study and meditate on the truths of the scriptures. That is their way of worship.

Others are intent on controlling the vital energy; so they practise breathing-exercises—inhalation, exhalation, and the stoppage of the breath. Others mortify their flesh by fasting, to weaken their sensual desires, and thus achieve self-control.

All these understand the meaning of sacrificial worship. Through worship, their sins are consumed away. They eat the food which has been blessed in the sacrifice. Thus they obtain immortality and reach eternal Brahman. He who does not worship God cannot be happy even in this world. What, then, can he expect from any other?

All these, and many other forms of worship are prescribed by the scriptures.

All of them involve the doing of some kind of action. When you fully understand this, you will be made free in Brahman.

The form of worship which consists in contemplating Brahman is superior to ritualistic worship with material offerings.

The reward of all action is to be found in enlightenment.

Those illumined souls who have realized the Truth will instruct you in the knowledge of Brahman, if you will prostrate yourself before them, question them and serve them as a disciple.

When you have reached enlightenment, ignorance will delude you no longer. In the light of that

* The path of Raja Yoga is said to have eight steps: (1) Practice of the moral virtues. (2) Regular habits of purity, contentment, study, austerity and self-surrender to God. (3) Posture. (4) Control of the vital energy by breathing-exercises. (5) Withdrawal of the mind from sense-objects. (6) Concentration. (7) Meditation. (8) Absorption in the consciousness of God.

knowledge you will see the entire creation within
your own Atman and in me.

And though you were the foulest of sinners,
This knowledge alone would carry you
Like a raft, over all your sin.

The blazing fire turns wood to ashes:
The fire of knowledge turns all karmas to ashes.

On earth there is no purifier
As great as this knowledge,
When a man is made perfect in yoga,
He knows its truth within his heart.
The man of faith,
Whose heart is devoted,
Whose senses are mastered:
He finds Brahman.
Enlightened, he passes
At once to the highest,
The peace beyond passion.

The ignorant, the faithless, the doubter
Goes to his destruction.
How shall he enjoy
This world, or the next,
Or any happiness?

When a man can act without desire,
Through practice of yoga;
When his doubts are torn to shreds,
Because he knows Brahman;
When his heart is poised
In the being of the Atman
No bonds can bind him.

Still I can see it:
A doubt that lingers
Deep in your heart
Brought forth by delusion.
You doubt the truth
Of the living Atman.

Where is your sword
Discrimination?
Draw it and slash
Delusion to pieces.
Then arise
O son of Bharata:
Take your stand
In Karma Yoga.

V. The Yoga of Renunciation

ARJUNA:

You speak so highly of the renunciation of action;
yet you ask me to follow the yoga of action. Now tell
me definitely: which of these is better?

SRI KRISHNA:

Action rightly renounced brings freedom:
Action rightly performed brings freedom:
Both are better
Than mere shunning of action.

When a man lacks lust and hatred,
His renunciation does not waver.
He neither longs for one thing

Nor loathes its opposite:
The chains of his delusion
Are soon cast off.

The yoga of action, say the ignorant,
Is different from the yoga of the knowledge
    of Brahman.

The wise see knowledge and action as one:
They see truly.
Take either path
And tread it to the end:
The end is the same.
There the followers of action
Meet the seekers after knowledge
In equal freedom.

It is hard to renounce action
Without following the yoga of action.
This yoga purifies
The man of meditation,
Bringing him soon to Brahman.

When the heart is made pure by that yoga,
When the body is obedient,
When the senses are mastered,
When man knows that his Atman
Is the Atman in all creatures,
Then let him act,
Untainted by action.

The illumined soul
Whose heart is Brahman's heart
Thinks always: 'I am doing nothing.'
No matter what he sees,
Hears, touches, smells, eats;
No matter whether he is moving,
Sleeping, breathing, speaking,

Excreting, or grasping something with his
        hand,
Or opening his eyes,
Or closing his eyes:
This he knows always:
'I am not seeing, I am not hearing:
It is the senses that see and hear
And touch the things of the senses.'

He puts aside desire,
Offering the act to Brahman.
The lotus leaf rests unwetted on water:
He rests on action, untouched by action.

To the follower of the yoga of action,
The body and the mind,
The sense-organs and the intellect
Are instruments only:
He knows himself other than the instrument
And thus his heart grows pure.

United with Brahman,
Cut free from the fruit of the act,
A man finds peace
In the work of the spirit.
Without Brahman,
Man is a prisoner,
Enslaved by action,
Dragged onward by desire.

Happy is that dweller
In the city of nine gates*
Whose discrimination
Has cut him free from his act:
He is not involved in action,
He does not involve others.

* The human body.

Do not say:
'God gave us this delusion.'
You dream you are the doer,
You dream that action is done,
You dream that action bears fruit.
It is your ignorance,
It is the world's delusion
That gives you these dreams.

The Lord is everywhere
And always perfect:
What does He care for man's sin
Or the righteousness of man?

The Atman is the light:
The light is covered by darkness:
This darkness is delusion:
That is why we dream.

When the light of the Atman
Drives out our darkness
That light shines forth from us,
A sun in splendour,
The revealed Brahman.

The devoted dwell with Him,
They know Him always
There in the heart,
Where action is not.
He is all their aim.
Made free by His Knowledge
From past uncleanness
Of deed or of thought,
They find the place of freedom,
The place of no return.*

* The state in which one is no longer subject to rebirth, because illumination has
been attained.

Seeing all things equal,
The enlightened may look
On the Brahmin, learned and gentle,
On the cow, on the elephant,
On the dog, on the eater of dogs.

Absorbed in Brahman
He overcomes the world
Even here, alive in the world.
Brahman is one,
Changeless, untouched by evil:
What home have we but Him?

The enlightened, the Brahman-abiding,
Calm-hearted, unbewildered,
Is neither elated by the pleasant
Nor saddened by the unpleasant.

His mind is dead
To the touch of the external:
It is alive
To the bliss of the Atman.
Because his heart knows Brahman
His happiness is for ever.

When senses touch objects
The pleasures therefrom
Are like wombs that bear sorrow.
They begin, they are ended:
They bring no delight to the wise.

Already, here on earth,
Before his departure,
Let man be the master
Of every impulse
Lust-begotten
Or fathered by anger:
Thus he finds Brahman,
Thus he is happy.

Only that yogi
Whose joy is inward,
Inward his peace,
And his vision inward
Shall come to Brahman
And know Nirvana.[1]

All consumed
Are their imperfections,
Doubts are dispelled,
Their senses mastered,
Their every action
Is wed to the welfare
Of fellow-creatures:
Such are the seers
Who enter Brahman
And know Nirvana.

Self-controlled,
Cut free from desire,
Curbing the heart
And knowing the Atman,
Man finds Nirvana
That is in Brahman,
Here and hereafter.

Shutting off sense
From what is outward,
Fixing the gaze
At the root of the eyebrows,[2]
Checking the breath-stream
In and outgoing
Within the nostrils,
Holding the senses,

[1] The state of union with Brahman.

[2] 'When the eyes are half closed in meditation, the eyeballs remain fixed and their gaze converges, as it were, between the eyebrows.'   *Swami Swarupananda*

Holding the intellect,
Holding the mind fast,
He who seeks freedom,
Thrusts fear aside,
Thrusts aside anger
And puts off desire:
Truly that man
Is made free for ever.

When thus he knows me
The end, the author
Of every offering
And all austerity,
Lord of the worlds
And the friend of all men:
O son of Kunti
Shall he not enter
The peace of my presence?

VI. The Yoga of Meditation

SRI KRISHNA:

He who does the task
Dictated by duty,
Caring nothing
For fruit of the action,
He is a yogi,
A true sannyasin.*
But he who follows
His vow to the letter
By mere refraining:

* Sannyasin: A monk.

Lighting no fire
At the ritual offering,
Making excuse
For avoidance of labour,
He is no yogi,
No true sannyasin.

For you must understand that what has been called yoga is really sannyasa*; since nobody can practise the yoga of action who is anxious about his future, or the results of his actions.

Let him who would climb
In meditation
To heights of the highest
Union with Brahman
Take for his path
The yoga of action:
Then when he nears
That height of oneness
His acts will fall from him,
His path will be tranquil.

For, when a man loses attachment to sense-objects and to action, when he renounces lustful anxiety and anxious lust, then he is said to have climbed to the height of union with Brahman.

What is man's will
And how shall he use it?
Let him put forth its power
To uncover the Atman
Not hide the Atman:

* Sannyasa: The formal vow of renunciation taken by a monk. In taking this vow he gives up the performance of the Vedic sacrificial rites.

Man's will is the only
Friend of the Atman:
His will is also
The Atman's enemy.

For when a man is self-controlled, his will is the Atman's friend. But the will of an uncontrolled man is hostile to the Atman, like an enemy.

That serene one
Absorbed in the Atman
Masters his will,
He knows no disquiet
In heat or in cold,
In pain or pleasure,
In honour, dishonour.

For when a man's heart has reached fulfilment through knowledge and personal experience of the truth of Brahman, he is never again moved by the things of the senses. Earth, stone and gold seem all alike to one who has mastered his senses. Such a yogi is said to have achieved union with Brahman.

He who regards
With an eye that is equal
Friends and comrades,
The foe and the kinsman,
The vile, the wicked,
The men who judge him,
And those who belong
To neither faction:
He is the greatest.

The yogi should retire into a solitary place, and live alone. He must exercise control over his mind and body. He must free himself from the hopes and possessions of this world. He should meditate on the Atman unceasingly.

The place where he sits should be firm, neither too high nor too low, and situated in a clean spot. He should first cover it with sacred grass, then with a deer skin; then lay a cloth over these.* As he sits there, he is to hold the senses and imagination in check, and keep the mind concentrated upon its object. If he practises meditation in this manner, his heart will become pure.

His posture will be motionless, with the body, head and neck held erect, and the vision indrawn, as if gazing at the tip of the nose. He must not look about him.

> So, with his heart serene and fearless,
> Firm in the vow of renunciation,
> Holding the mind from its restless roaming,
> Now let him struggle to reach my oneness,
> Ever-absorbed, his eyes on me always,
> His prize, his purpose.

If a yogi has perfect control over his mind, and struggles continually in this way to unite himself with Brahman, he will come at last to the crowning peace of Nirvana, the peace that is in me.

Yoga is not for the man who overeats, or for him who fasts excessively. It is not for him who sleeps too much, or for the keeper of exaggerated vigils. Let a man be moderate in his eating and his recreation, moderately active, moderate in sleep and in wakefulness. He will find that yoga takes away all his unhappiness.

* The choice of materials is traditional, but not important for the spiritual aspirant of to-day. Any convenient seat will do.

When can a man be said to have achieved union with Brahman? When his mind is under perfect control and freed from all desires, so that he becomes absorbed in the Atman, and nothing else. 'The light of a lamp does not flicker in a windless place': that is the simile which describes a yogi of one-pointed mind, who meditates upon the Atman. When, through the practise of yoga, the mind ceases its restless movements, and becomes still, he realizes the Atman. It satisfies him entirely. Then he knows that infinite happiness which can be realized by the purified heart but is beyond the grasp of the senses. He stands firm in this realization. Because of it, he can never again wander from the inmost truth of his being.

> Now that he holds it
> He knows this treasure
> Above all others:
> Faith so certain
> Shall never be shaken
> By heaviest sorrow.

To achieve this certainty is to know the real meaning of the word yoga. It is the breaking of contact with pain. You must practise this yoga resolutely, without losing heart. Renounce all your desires, for ever. They spring from wilfulness. Use your discrimination to restrain the whole pack of the scattering senses.

Patiently, little by little, a man must free himself from all mental distractions, with the aid of the intelligent will. He must fix his mind upon the Atman, and never think of anything else. No matter where the restless and the unquiet mind wanders, it must be drawn back and made to submit to the Atman only.

Utterly quiet,
Made clean of passion,
The mind of the yogi
Knows that Brahman,
His bliss is the highest.

Released from evil
His mind is constant
In contemplation:
The way is easy,
Brahman has touched him,
That bliss is boundless.

His heart is with Brahman,
His eye in all things
Sees only Brahman
Equally present,
Knows his own Atman
In every creature,
And all creation
Within that Atman.

That yogi sees me in all things, and all things
within me. He never loses sight of me, nor I of him.
He is established in union with me, and worships me
devoutly in all beings. That yogi abides in me, no
matter what his mode of life.

Who burns with the bliss
And suffers the sorrow
Of every creature
Within his own heart,
Making his own
Each bliss and each sorrow:
Him I hold highest
Of all the yogis.

ARJUNA:

Krishna, you describe this yoga as a life of union
with Brahman. But I do not see how this can be
permanent. The mind is so very restless.

> Restless man's mind is,
> So strongly shaken
> In the grip of the senses:
> Gross and grown hard
> With stubborn desire
> For what is worldly.
> How shall he tame it?
> Truly, I think
> The wind is no wilder.

SRI KRISHNA:

Yes, Arjuna, the mind is restless, no doubt, and hard
to subdue. But it can be brought under control by
constant practice, and by the exercise of dispassion.
Certainly, if a man has no control over his ego, he
will find this yoga difficult to master. But a self-
controlled man can master it, if he struggles hard,
and uses the right means.

ARJUNA:

Suppose a man has faith, but does not struggle hard
enough? His mind wanders away from the practice
of yoga and he fails to reach perfection. What will
become of him then?

When a man goes astray from the path to Brahman, he has missed both lives, the worldly and the
spiritual. He has no support anywhere. Is he not lost,
as a broken cloud is lost in the sky?

This is the doubt that troubles me, Krishna; and
only you can altogether remove it from my mind.
Let me hear your answer.

SRI KRISHNA:

No, my son. That man is not lost, either in this world or the next. No one who seeks Brahman ever comes to an evil end.

Even if a man falls away from the practice of yoga, he will still win the heaven of the doers of good deeds, and dwell there many long years. After that, he will be reborn into the home of pure and prosperous parents. He may even be born into a family of illumined yogis. But such a birth in this world is more difficult to obtain.

He will then regain that spiritual discernment which he acquired in his former body; and so will strive harder than ever for perfection. Because of his practices in the previous life, he will be driven on toward union with Brahman, even in spite of himself. For the man who has once asked the way to Brahman goes further than any mere fulfiller of the Vedic rituals. By struggling hard, and cleansing himself of all impurities, that yogi will move gradually toward perfection through many births, and reach the highest goal at last.

> Great is that yogi who seeks to be with
>   Brahman,
> Greater than those who mortify the body,
> Greater than the learned,
> Greater than the doers of good works:
> Therefore, Arjuna, become a yogi.
>
> He gives me all his heart,
> He worships me in faith and love:
> That yogi, above every other,
> I call my very own.

VII. Knowledge and Experience

Devote your whole mind to me, and practise yoga. Take me for your only refuge. I will tell you how, by doing this, you can know me in my total reality, without any shadow of doubt. I will give you all this knowledge, and direct spiritual experience, besides. When a man has that, nothing else in this world remains to be known.

> Who cares to seek
> For that perfect freedom?
> One man, perhaps,
> In many thousands.
> Then tell me how many
> Of those who seek freedom
> Shall know the total
> Truth of my being?
> Perhaps one only.

My Prakriti is of eightfold composition: earth, water, fire, air, ether, mind, intellect and ego. You must understand that behind this, and distinct from it, is That which is the principle of consciousness in all beings, and the source of life in all. It sustains the universe.

> Know this my Parkriti
> United with me:
> The womb of all beings.
> I am the birth of this cosmos:
> Its dissolution also.

I am He who causes:
No other beside me.
Upon me, these worlds are held
Like pearls strung on a thread.

I am the essence of the waters,
The shining of the sun and the moon:
OM in all the Vedas,
The word that is God.
It is I who resound in the ether
And am potent in man.
I am the sacred smell of the earth,
The light of the fire,
Life of all lives,
Austerity of ascetics.

Know me, eternal seed
Of everything that grows:
The intelligence of those who understand,
The vigour of the active.
In the strong, I am strength
Unhindered by lust
And the objects of craving:
I am all that a man may desire
Without transgressing
The law of his nature.

You must know that whatever belongs to the
states of sattwa, rajas and tamas, proceeds from me.
They are contained in me, but I am not in them. The
entire world is deluded by the moods and mental
states which are the expression of these three gunas.
That is why the world fails to recognize me as I
really am. I stand apart from them all, supreme and
deathless.

How hard to break through
Is this, my Maya,
Made of the gunas!
But he who takes refuge
Within me only
Shall pass beyond Maya:
He, and no other.

The evil-doers
Turn not toward me:
These are deluded,
Sunk low among mortals.
Their judgment is lost
In the maze of Maya,
Until the heart
Is human no longer:
Changed within
To the heart of a devil.

Among those who are purified by their good
deeds, there are four kinds of men who worship me:
the world-weary, the seeker for knowledge, the
seeker for happiness and the man of spiritual discrimination. The man of discrimination is the highest of these. He is continually united with me. He
devotes himself to me always, and to no other. For
I am very dear to that man, and he is dear to me.

Certainly, all these are noble:
But the man of discrimination
I see as my very Self.
For he alone loves me
Because I am myself:
The last and only goal
Of his devoted heart.

Through many a long life
His discrimination ripens:
He makes me his refuge,
Knows that Brahman is all.
How rare are such great ones!

Men whose discrimination has been blunted by worldly desires, establish this or that ritual or cult and resort to various deities, according to the impulse of their inborn natures. But it does not matter what deity a devotee chooses to worship. If he has faith, I make his faith unwavering. Endowed with the faith I give him, he worships that deity, and gets from it everything he prays for. In reality, I alone am the giver.

But these men of small understanding only pray for what is transient and perishable. The worshippers of the devas will go to the devas. So, also, my devotees will come to me.

Thus think the ignorant: that I, the unmanifest,
Am become man. They do not know my nature
That is one with Brahman, changeless,
        superhuman.

Veiled in my Maya, I am not shown to many.
How shall this world, bewildered by delusion,
Recognize me, who am not born and change
        not?

I know all beings, Arjuna: past, present and to come. But no one knows me.

All living creatures are led astray as soon as they are born, by the delusion that this relative world is real. This delusion arises from their own desire and hatred. But the doers of good deeds, whose bad karma is exhausted, are freed from this delusion about the relative world. They hold firmly to their vows, and worship me.

Men take refuge in me, to escape from their fear of old age and death. Thus they come to know Brahman, and the entire nature of the Atman, and the creative energy which is in Brahman. Knowing me, they understand the nature of the relative world and the individual man, and of God who presides over all action. Even at the hour of death, they continue to know me thus. In that hour, their whole consciousness is made one with mine.

VIII. The Way To Eternal Brahman

ARJUNA:

Tell me, Krishna, what Brahman is. What is the Atman, and what is the creative energy of Brahman? Explain the nature of this relative world, and of the individual man.

Who is God who presides over action in this body, and how does He dwell here? How are you revealed at the hour of death to those whose consciousness is united with you?

SRI KRISHNA:

Brahman is that which is immutable, and independent of any cause but Itself. When we consider Brahman as lodged within the individual being, we call Him the Atman. The creative energy of Brahman is that which causes all existences to come into being.

The nature of the relative world is mutability. The nature of the individual man is his consciousness of ego. I alone am God who presides over action, here in this body.

At the hour of death, when a man leaves his body, he must depart with his consciousness absorbed in me. Then he will be united with me. Be certain of that. Whatever a man remembers at the last, when he is leaving the body, will be realized by him in the hereafter; because that will be what his mind has most constantly dwelt on, during this life.

Therefore you must remember me at all times, and do your duty. If your mind and heart are set upon me constantly, you will come to me. Never doubt this.

Make a habit of practising meditation, and do not let your mind be distracted. In this way you will come finally to the Lord, who is the light-giver, the highest of the high.

He is all-knowing God, lord of the emperors,
Ageless, subtler far than mind's inmost subtlety,
Universal sustainer,
Shining sunlike, self-luminous.

What fashion His form has, who shall conceive
    of it?
He dwells beyond delusion, the dark of Maya.
On Him let man meditate
Always, for then at the last hour
Of going hence from his body he will be strong
In the strength of this yoga, faithfully followed:
The mind is firm, and the heart
So full, it hardly holds its love.

Thus he will take his leave: and now, with the
    life-force
Indrawn utterly, held fast between the
    eyebrows,
He goes forth to find his Lord,
That light-giver, who is greatest.

Now I will tell you briefly about the nature of
Him who is called the deathless by those seers who
truly understand the Vedas. Devotees enter into
Him when the bonds of their desire are broken. To
reach this goal, they practise control of the passions.

When a man leaves his body and departs,[1] he
must close all the doors of the senses. Let him hold
the mind firmly within the shrine of the heart, and
fix the life-force between the eyebrows. Then let
him take refuge in steady concentration, uttering
the sacred syllable OM and meditating upon me.
Such a man reaches the highest goal. When a yogi
has meditated upon me unceasingly for many years,
with an undistracted mind, I am easy of access to
him, because he is always absorbed in me.

Great souls who find me have found the highest
perfection. They are no longer reborn into this condition of transience and pain.

All the worlds, and even the heavenly realm of
Brahma,[2] are subject to the laws of rebirth. But, for
the man who comes to me, there is no returning.

---

[1] According to yoga technique, the yogi must employ a special method of leaving
the body at death. First, the vital force is drawn up the sushumna, the central
spinal passage, and gathered in the brain, 'between the eyebrows.' The yogi then
leaves the body through an aperture in the centre of the brain, called the
sahashrara.

[2] Brahma (not to be confused with Brahman) is God in the aspect of creator—
one of the Hindu Trinity, with Vishnu, the preserver, and Shiva, the dissolver.
Also see Appendix I.

According to Hindu mythology, the worlds are variously classified as three,
seven or fourteen. The Brahma-Loka (realm of Brahma) is said to be the highest.

There is day, also, and night in the universe:
The wise know this, declaring the day of
    Brahma
A thousand ages in span
And the night a thousand ages.[1]

Day dawns, and all those lives that lay hidden
    asleep
Come forth and show themselves, mortally
    manifest:
Night falls, and all are dissolved
Into the sleeping germ of life.

Thus they are seen, O Prince, and appear
    unceasingly,
Dissolving with the dark, and with day
    returning
Back to the new birth, new death:
All helpless. They do what they must.

But behind the manifest and the unmanifest, there is another Existence, which is eternal and changeless. This is not dissolved in the general cosmic dissolution. It has been called the unmanifest, the imperishable. To reach it is said to be the greatest of all achievements. It is my highest state of being. Those who reach It are not reborn. That highest state of being can only be achieved through devotion to Him in whom all creatures exist, and by whom this universe is pervaded.

I show you two paths.[2]
Let a yogi choose either
When he leaves this body:
The path that leads back to birth,
The path of no return.

[1] See Appendix I, page 132.

[2] The 'path of no return' is called in the Upanishads the Deva Yana, 'the path of the bright ones,' who are liberated from rebirth. The path that leads back to birth is the Pitri Yana, the 'path of the fathers,' who reach the 'lunar light' (a paradise subject to the laws of time) and must ultimately be reborn.

There is the path of light,
Of fire and day,
The path of the moon's bright fortnight
And the six months' journey
Of the sun to the north:
The knower of Brahman
Who takes this path
Goes to Brahman:
He does not return.

There is the path of night and smoke,
The path of the moon's dark fortnight
And the six months' journey
Of the sun to the south:
The yogi who takes this path
Will reach the lunar light: *
This path leads back
To human birth, at last.

These two paths, the bright and the dark, may
be said to have existed in this world of change from
a time without any beginning. By the one, a man
goes to the place of no return. By the other, he
comes back to human birth. No yogi who knows
these two paths is ever misled. Therefore, Arjuna,
you must be steadfast in yoga, always.

The scriptures declare that merit can be acquired
by studying the Vedas, performing ritualistic sacrifices, practising austerities and giving alms. But the
yogi who has understood this teaching of mine will
gain more than any who do these things. He will
reach that universal source, which is the uttermost
abode of God.

* Fire, light, smoke, night, etc., probably represent stages of the soul's experience
after death. Thus, light may symbolize knowledge; and smoke, ignorance.

IX. The Yoga of Mysticism

SRI KRISHNA:

Since you accept me
And do not question,
Now I shall tell you
That innermost secret:
Knowledge of God
Which is nearer than knowing,
Open vision
Direct and instant.
Understand this
And be free for ever
From birth and dying
With all their evil.

This is the knowledge
Above all other:
Purifier
And king of secrets,
Only made plain
To the eye of the mystic.
Great is its virtue,
Its practice easy:
Thus man is brought
To truth eternal.

Those without faith
In this, my knowledge,
Shall fail to find me:
Back they must turn
To the mortal pathway,
Subject still
To birth and to dying.

This entire universe is pervaded by me, in that eternal form of mine which is not manifest to the senses. Although I am not within any creature, all creatures exist within me. I do not mean that they exist within me physically. That is my divine mystery. You must try to understand its nature. My Being sustains all creatures and brings them to birth, but has no physical contact with them.

For, as the vast air, wandering world-wide,
Remains within the ether always,
So these, my wandering creatures,
Are always within me.

These, when the round of ages is accomplished,
I gather back to the seed of their becoming:
These I send forth again
At the hour of creation.

Helpless all, for Maya is their master,
And I, their Lord, the master of this Maya:
Ever and again, I send these multitudes
Forth from my Being.

How shall these acts bind me, who am
    indifferent
To the fruit they bear? For my spirit
Stands apart, watching over
Maya, the maker.

Maya makes all things: what moves, what is
    unmoving.
O son of Kunti, that is why the world spins,
Turning its wheel through birth
And through destruction.

Fools pass blindly by the place of my dwelling
Here in the human form, and of my majesty
They know nothing at all,
Who am the Lord, their soul.

Vain is their hope, and in vain their labour,
      their knowledge:
All their understanding is but bewilderment;
Their nature has fallen into the madness
Of the fiends and monsters.

Great in soul are they who become what is
      godlike:
They alone know me, the origin, the deathless:
They offer me the homage
Of an unwavering mind.

Praising my might with heart and lips for ever,
Striving for the virtue that wins me, and
      steadfast
In all their vows, they worship adoring,
One with me always.
Others worship me, knowing Brahman in all
      things:
Some see me one with themselves, or separate:
Some bow to the countless gods that are only
My million faces.

Rites that the Vedas ordain, and the rituals
      taught by the scriptures:
All these am I, and the offering made to the
      ghosts of the fathers,
Herbs of healing and food, the mantram,* the
      clarified butter:
I the oblation and I the flame into which it is
      offered.

* Name, or names, of God, which the devotee must repeat and meditate upon. An
individual mantram is given by the teacher to each of his disciples at the time
of initiation.

I am the sire of the world, and this world's
   mother and grandsire:
I am He who awards to each the fruit of his
   action:
I make all things clean, I am OM, I am absolute
   knowledge:
I am also the Vedas—the Sama, the Rik and the
   Yajus.
I am the end of the path, the witness, the Lord,
   the sustainer:
I am the place of abode, the beginning, the
   friend and the refuge:
I am the breaking-apart, and the storehouse of
   life's dissolution:
I lie under the seen, of all creatures the seed
   that is changeless.

I am the heat of the sun; and the heat of the
   fire am I also:
Life eternal and death. I let loose the rain, or
   withhold it.
Arjuna, I am the cosmos revealed, and its germ
   that lies hidden.

> They that are versed
> In the triple Veda,
> Worshipping me
> With the rites appointed,
> Drinking the wine
> Of the gods' communion,
> Cleansed from their sinning:
> These men pray
> For passage to heaven,
> Thus attaining
> The realm of Indra,
> Home of the happy;
> There they delight
> In celestial pleasures.

Pleasures more spacious
Than any earthly
They taste awhile,
Till the merit that won them
Is all exhausted:
Then they return
To the world of mortals.

Thus go the righteous
Who follow the road
 Of the triple Veda
In formal observance;
Hungry still
For the food of the senses,
Drawn by desire
To endless returning.

But if a man will worship me, and meditate upon me with an undistracted mind, devoting every moment to me, I shall supply all his needs, and protect his possessions from loss. Even those who worship other deities, and sacrifice to them with faith in their hearts, are really worshipping me, though with a mistaken approach. For I am the only enjoyer and the only God of all sacrifices. Nevertheless, such men must return to life on earth, because they do not recognize me in my true nature.

Those who sacrifice to the various deities, will go to those deities. The ancestor-worshippers will go to their ancestors. Those who worship elemental powers and spirits will go to them. So, also, my devotees will come to me.

Whatever man gives me
In true devotion:
Fruit or water,

A leaf, a flower:
I will accept it.
That gift is love,
His heart's dedication.

Whatever your action,
Food or worship;
Whatever the gift
That you give to another;
Whatever you vow
To the work of the spirit:
O son of Kunti,
Lay these also
As offerings before me.

Thus you will free yourself from both the good and the evil effects of your actions. Offer up everything to me. If your heart is united with me, you will be set free from karma even in this life, and come to me at the last.

My face is equal
To all creation,
Loving no one
Nor hating any.

Nevertheless,
My devotees dwell
Within me always:
I also show forth
And am seen within them.

Though a man be soiled
With the sins of a lifetime,
Let him but love me,
Rightly resolved,
In utter devotion:

> I see no sinner,
> That man is holy.
> Holiness soon
> Shall refashion his nature
> To peace eternal;
> O son of Kunti,
> Of this be certain:
> The man that loves me,
> He shall not perish.

Even those who belong to the lower castes—women, Vaishyas,* and Sudras too—can reach the highest spiritual realization, if they will take refuge in me. Need I tell you, then, that this is also true of the holy Brahmins and pious philosopher-kings?

You find yourself in this transient, joyless world. Turn from it, and take your delight in me. Fill your heart and mind with me, adore me, make all your acts an offering to me, bow down to me in self-surrender. If you set your heart upon me thus, and take me for your ideal above all others, you will come into my Being.

X. Divine Glory

SRI KRISHNA:

> Once more, warrior,
> Hear this highest
> Word of my wisdom:
> Wishing your welfare,
> To you I teach it
> Since your heart
> Delights in the telling.

---

* The four Hindu castes are: Brahmins (the priests), Kshatriyas (the warriors), Vaishyas (the merchants) and Sudras (the servants). Compare Chapter XVIII page 125, where the caste-names are used with a more psychological significance, and have been translated accordingly.

How shall the mighty
Seers or the devas
Know my beginning?
I am the origin,
I the sustainer
Of seers and devas.

Who knows me birthless,
Never-beginning,
Lord of the worlds;
He alone among mortals
Is stainless of sin,
Unvexed by delusion.

All that makes Man
In his many natures:
Knowledge and power
Of understanding
Unclouded by error,
Truth, forbearance,
Calm of spirit,
Control of senses,
Happiness, sorrow,
Birth and destruction,
What fears, what is fearless,
What harms no creature,
The mind unshaken,
The heart contented,
The will austere,
The hand of the giver,
Fame and honour
And infamy also:
It is by me only
That these are allotted.
Forth from my thought
Came the seven Sages,

The Ancient Four
And at last the Manus:
Thus I gave birth
To the first begetters
Of all earth's children.

Who truly knows me,
In manifold Being
Everywhere present
And all-prevailing,
Dwells in my yoga
That shall not be shaken:
Of this be certain.

I am where all things began, the issuing-forth of the
creatures,
Known to the wise in their love when they worship
with hearts overflowing:

Mind and sense are absorbed, I alone am the theme
of their discourse:
Thus delighting each other, they live in bliss and
contentment.
Always aware of their Lord are they, and ever
devoted:
Therefore the strength of their thought is illumined
and guided toward me.

There in the ignorant heart where I dwell, by the
grace of my mercy,
I am knowledge, that brilliant lamp, dispelling its
darkness.

ARJUNA:

You are Brahman, the highest abode, the utterly
holy:
All the sages proclaim you eternal, Lord of the
devas:

Saintly Narada knew you the birthless, the everywhere present:
Devala echoed your praise; Asita, too, and Vyasa:*
Now I also have heard, for to me your own lips have
 confirmed it,
Krishna, this is the truth that you tell: my heart bids
 me believe you.

God of gods, Lord of the world, Life's Source, O
 King of all creatures:
How shall deva or titan know all the extent of your
 glory?
You alone know what you are, by the light of your
 innermost nature.
Therefore teach me now, and hold back no word
 in the telling,
All the sum of your shapes by which the three
 worlds are pervaded;
Tell me how you will make yourself known to my
 meditation;
Show me beneath what form and disguise I must
 learn to behold you;
Number them all, your heavenly powers, your mani-
 festations:
Speak, for each word is immortal nectar; I never
 grow weary.

SRI KRISHNA:

O Arjuna, I will indeed make known to you my
divine manifestations; but I shall name the chief
of these, only. For, of the lesser variations in all
their detail, there is no end.

 I am the Atman that dwells in the heart of every
mortal creature: I am the beginning, the life-span,
and the end of all.

* Ancient sages.

I am Vishnu: I am the radiant sun among the light-givers: I am Marichi, the wind-god: among the stars of night, I am the moon.

I am the Sama Veda: I am Indra, king of heaven: of sense-organs, I am the mind: I am consciousness in the living.

I am Shiva: I am the Lord of all riches: I am the spirit of fire: I am Meru, among the mountain peaks.

Know me as Brihaspati, leader of the high priests, and as Skanda, the warrior-chief. I am the ocean among the waters.

I am Bhrigu, the great seer: among words, I am the sacred syllable OM: I am the vow of japam: *
I am Himalaya among the things that cannot be moved.

I am the holy fig tree: I am Narada, the godly sage, Chitraratha, the celestial musician, and Kapila among the perfected souls.

Among horses, you may know me as Uchchaishrava, who was brought forth from the sea of nectar: I am Airavata among royal elephants: I am king among men.

Of weapons, I am God's thunderbolt: I am Kamadhenu, the heavenly cow: I am the love-god, begetter of children: I am Vasuki, god of snakes.

I am Ananta, the holy serpent: of water beings, I am Varuna: Aryaman among the Fathers: I am Death, who distributes the fruit of all action.

I am Prahlada, the giant: among those who measure, I am Time: I am the lion among beasts: Vishnu's eagle among the birds.

Among purifiers, I am the wind: I am Rama among the warriors: the shark among fish: Ganges among the rivers.

I am the beginning, the middle and the end in

* The practice of repeating a mantram (name of God). See note on Chapter IX, page 81.

creation: I am the knowledge of things spiritual: I am the logic of those who debate.

In the alphabet, I am A: among compounds, the copulative: I am Time without end: I am the Sustainer: my face is everywhere.

I am death that snatches all: I, also, am the source of all that shall be born: I am glory, prosperity, beautiful speech, memory, intelligence, steadfastness and forgiveness.

I am the great Sama of the Vedic hymns, and the Gayatri among poetic metres: of the months, I am Margashirsha: * of seasons, the time of flowers.

I am the dice-play of the cunning: I am the strength of the strong: I am triumph and perseverance: I am the purity of the good.

I am Krishna among the Vrishnis, Arjuna among the Pandavas, Vyasa among the sages, Ushanas among the illumined poets.

I am the sceptre and the mastery of those who rule, the policy of those who seek to conquer: I am the silence of things secret: I am the knowledge of the knower.

O Arjuna, I am the divine seed of all lives. In this world, nothing animate or inanimate exists without me.

There is no limit to my divine manifestations, nor can they be numbered, O foe-consumer. What I have described to you are only a few of my countless forms.

Whatever in this world is powerful, beautiful or glorious, that you may know to have come forth from a fraction of my power and glory.

But what need have you, Arjuna, to know this huge variety? Know only that I exist, and that one atom of myself sustains the universe.

* A month of the Hindu year, including parts of November and December.

XI. The Vision of God in His Universal Form

ARJUNA:

By your grace, you have taught me the truth about the Atman. Your words are mystic and sublime. They have dispelled my ignorance.

From you, whose eyes are like the lotus-flowers, I have learnt in detail of the origin and dissolution of creatures, and of your own infinite glory.

O Supreme Lord, you are as you describe yourself to be: I do not doubt that. Nevertheless, I long to behold your divine Form.

If you find me worthy of that vision, then reveal to me, O Master of yogis, your changeless Atman.

SRI KRISHNA:

Behold, O Prince, my divine forms, hundreds upon thousands, various in kind, various in colour and in shape.

Behold the Adityas, and the Vasus, and the Rudras, and the Aswins, and the Maruts.* Behold many wonders, O Descendant of Bharata, that no man has seen before.

O conqueror of sloth, this very day you shall behold the whole universe with all things animate and inert made one within this body of mine. And whatever else you desire to see, that you shall see also.

But you cannot see me thus with those human eyes. Therefore, I give you divine sight. Behold— this is my yoga power.

SANJAYA:

Then, O King, when he had spoken these words, Sri Krishna, Master of all yogis, revealed to Arjuna his

* Various classes of celestial beings.

transcendent, divine Form, speaking from innumerable mouths, seeing with a myriad eyes, of many marvellous aspects, adorned with countless divine ornaments, brandishing all kinds of heavenly weapons, wearing celestial garlands and the raiment of paradise, anointed with perfumes of heavenly fragrance, full of revelations, resplendent, boundless, of ubiquitous regard.

Suppose a thousand suns should rise together into the sky: such is the glory of the Shape of Infinite God.

Then the son of Pandu beheld the entire universe, in all its multitudinous diversity, lodged as one being within the body of the God of gods.

Then was Arjuna, that lord of mighty riches, overcome with wonder. His hair stood erect. He bowed low before God in adoration, and clasped his hands, and spoke:

ARJUNA:

Ah, my God, I see all gods within your body;
Each in his degree, the multitude of creatures;
See Lord Brahma throned upon the lotus;
See all the sages, and the holy serpents.

Universal Form, I see you without limit,
Infinite of arms, eyes, mouths and bellies—
See, and find no end, midst, or beginning.

Crowned with diadems, you wield the mace and
    discus,
Shining every way—the eyes shrink from your
    splendour
Brilliant like the sun; like fire, blazing, boundless.

You are all we know, supreme, beyond man's
    measure,

This world's sure-set plinth and refuge never shaken,
Guardian of eternal law, life's Soul undying.
Birthless, deathless; yours the strength titanic,
Million-armed, the sun and moon your eyeballs,
Fiery-faced, you blast the world to ashes,

Fill the sky's four corners, span the chasm
Sundering heaven from earth. Superb and awful
Is your Form that makes the three worlds tremble.

Into you, the companies of devas
Enter with clasped hands, in dread and wonder.
Crying 'Peace,' the Rishis and the Siddhas
Sing your praise with hymns of adoration.

Adityas and Rudras, Sadhyas, Viswas, Aswins,
Maruts and Vasus, the hosts of the Gandharvas,
Yakshas, Asuras, Ushmapas and Siddhas—
All of them gaze upon you in amazement.

At the sight of this, your Shape stupendous
Full of mouths and eyes, feet, thighs and bellies,
Terrible with fangs, O mighty master,
All the worlds are fear-struck, even as I am.

When I see you, Vishnu, omnipresent,
Shouldering the sky, in hues of rainbow,
With your mouths agape and flame-eyes staring—
All my peace is gone; my heart is troubled.

Now with frightful tusks your mouths are gnashing,
Flaring like the fires of Doomsday morning—
North, south, east and west seem all confounded—
Lord of devas, world's abode, have mercy!

Dhritarashtra's offspring, many a monarch,
Bhisma, Drona, and the son of Karna,
There they go—with our own warriors also—
Hurrying to your jaws, wide-fanged and hideous—
See where mangled heads lie crushed between them!

Swift as many rivers streaming to the ocean,
Rush the heroes to your fiery gullets:
Mothlike, to meet the flame of their destruction,
Headlong these plunge into you, and perish.

Licking with your burning tongues, devouring
All the worlds, you probe the heights of heaven
With intolerable beams, O Vishnu.

Tell me who you are, and were from the beginning,
You of aspect grim, O God of gods, be gracious.
Take my homage, Lord. From me your ways are
    hidden.

SRI KRISHNA:

I am come as Time, the waster of the peoples,
Ready for that hour that ripens to their ruin.
All these hosts must die; strike, stay your hand—no
    matter.

Therefore, strike. Win kingdom, wealth and glory.
Arjuna, arise, O ambidextrous bowman.
Seem to slay. By me these men are slain already.

You but smite the dead, the doom-devoted heroes,
Jayadratha, Drona, Bhisma, Karna.
Fight, and have no fear. The foe is yours to conquer.

SANJAYA:

After Arjuna had heard these words of the Lord
Krishna, he folded his palms and bowed down,
trembling. Prostrating himself, with great fear, he
addressed Krishna once more, in a choking voice:

ARJUNA:

Well it is the world delights to do you honour!
At the sight of you, O master of the senses,
Demons scatter every way in terror,
And the hosts of Siddhas bow adoring.

Mightiest, how should they indeed withhold their
    homage?
O Prime Cause of all, even Brahma the Beginner—
Deathless, world's abode, the Lord of devas,
You are what is not, what is, and what transcends
    them.

You are first and highest in heaven, O ancient Spirit.
It is within you the cosmos rests in safety.
You are known and knower, goal of all our striving.
Endless in your change, you body forth creation.

Lord of fire and death, of wind and moon and
    waters,
Father of the born, and this world's father's Father.
Hail, all hail to you—a thousand salutations.

Take our salutations, Lord, from every quarter,
Infinite of might and boundless in your glory,
You are all that is, since everywhere we find you.

Carelessly I called you 'Krishna' and 'my comrade,'
Took undying God for friend and fellow-mortal,
Overbold with love, unconscious of your greatness.

Often I would jest, familiar, as we feasted
Midst the throng, or walked, or lay at rest together:
Did my words offend? Forgive me, Lord Eternal.

Author of this world, the unmoved and the moving,
You alone are fit for worship, you the highest.
Where in the three worlds shall any find your equal?

Therefore I bow down, prostrate and ask for pardon:
Now forgive me, God, as friend forgives his
         comrade,
Father forgives son, and man his dearest lover.

I have seen what no man ever saw before me:
Deep is my delight, but still my dread is greater.
Show me now your other Form, O Lord, be gracious.

Thousand-membered, Universal Being,
Show me now the Shape I knew of old, the four-
         armed,*
With your diadem and mace, the discus-bearer.

SRI KRISHNA:

This my Form of fire, world-wide, supreme,
         primeval,
Manifest by yoga power, alone of all men,
Arjuna, I showed to you because I love you.

Neither through sacrifice, nor study of the Vedas,
Nor strict austerities, nor alms, nor rituals,
Shall this my Shape be viewed by any mortal,
Other than you, O hero of the Pandus.

Now you need fear no more, nor be bewildered,
Seeing me so terrible. Be glad, take courage.
Look, here am I, transformed, as first you knew me.

SANJAYA:

Having spoken thus to Arjuna, Krishna appeared in
his own shape. The Great-Souled One, assuming
once more his mild and pleasing form, brought
peace to him in his terror.

---

* The only explanation of this passage seems to be that Arjuna is asking Sri
Krishna to assume the shape of his chosen deity. Vishnu—since it cannot mean
that Krishna had four arms while in his human shape. If this interpretation is
correct, we may assume that God took on the four-armed shape of Vishnu for a
moment, before reappearing as Krishna. As has been stated elsewhere, Krishna
was regarded as an incarnation of Vishnu.

ARJUNA:

O Krishna, now I see your pleasant human form,
I am myself again.

SRI KRISHNA:

That Shape of mine which you have seen is very
difficult to behold. Even the devas themselves are
always longing to see it. Neither by study of the
Vedas, nor by austerities, nor by alms-giving, nor
by rituals can I be seen as you have seen me. But
by single-minded and intense devotion, that Form
of mine may be completely known, and seen, and
entered into, O Consumer of the foe.

Whosoever works for me alone, makes me his only
goal and is devoted to me, free from attachment,
and without hatred toward any creature—that man,
O Prince, shall enter into me.

XII. The Yoga of Devotion

ARJUNA:

Some worship you with steadfast love. Others worship God the unmanifest and changeless. Which
kind of devotee has the greater understanding of
yoga?

SRI KRISHNA:

Those whose minds are fixed on me in steadfast
love, worshipping me with absolute faith. I consider
them to have the greater understanding of yoga.

As for those others, the devotees of God the unmanifest, indefinable and changeless, they worship
that which is omnipresent, constant, eternal, beyond
thought's compass, never to be moved. They hold

all the senses in check. They are tranquil-minded,
and devoted to the welfare of humanity. They see
the Atman in every creature. They also will certainly
come to me.

But the devotees of the unmanifest have a harder
task, because the unmanifest is very difficult for
embodied souls to realize.

> Quickly I come
> To those who offer me
> Every action,
> Worship me only,
> Their dearest delight,
> With devotion undaunted.

> Because they love me
> These are my bondsmen
> And I shall save them
> From mortal sorrow
> And all the waves
> Of Life's deathly ocean.

> Be absorbed in me,
> Lodge your mind in me:
> Thus you shall dwell in me,
> Do not doubt it,
> Here and hereafter.

If you cannot become absorbed in me, then try
to reach me by repeated concentration. If you lack
the strength to concentrate, then devote yourself
to works which will please me. For, by working
for my sake only, you will achieve perfection. If you
cannot even do this, then surrender yourself to me
altogether. Control the lusts of your heart, and renounce the fruits of every action.

Concentration which is practised with discernment is certainly better than the mechanical repetition of a ritual or a prayer. Absorption in God—to live with Him and be one with Him always—is even better than concentration. But renunciation brings instant peace to the spirit.

A man should not hate any living creature. Let him be friendly and compassionate to all. He must free himself from the delusion of 'I' and 'mine.' He must accept pleasure and pain with equal tranquillity. He must be forgiving, ever-contented, self-controlled, united constantly with me in his meditation. His resolve must be unshakable. He must be dedicated to me in intellect and in mind. Such a devotee is dear to me.

He neither molests his fellow men, nor allows himself to become disturbed by the world. He is no longer swayed by joy and envy, anxiety and fear. Therefore he is dear to me.

He is pure, and independent of the body's desire. He is able to deal with the unexpected: prepared for everything, unperturbed by anything. He is neither vain nor anxious about the results of his actions. Such a devotee is dear to me.

He does not desire or rejoice in what is pleasant. He does not dread what is unpleasant, or grieve over it. He remains unmoved by good or evil fortune. Such a devotee is dear to me.

His attitude is the same toward friend and foe. He is indifferent to honour and insult, heat and cold, pleasure and pain. He is free from attachment. He values praise and blame equally. He can control his speech. He is content with whatever he gets. His home is everywhere and nowhere. His mind is fixed upon me, and his heart is full of devotion. He is dear to me.

This true wisdom I have taught will lead you to immortality. The faithful practise it with devotion, taking me for their highest aim. To me they surrender heart and mind. They are exceedingly dear to me.

XIII. The Field and Its Knower

ARJUNA:

And now, Krishna, I wish to learn about Prakriti and Brahman, the Field and the Knower of the Field. What is knowledge? What is it that has to be known?

SRI KRISHNA:

This body is called the Field, because a man sows seeds of action in it, and reaps their fruits. Wise men say that the Knower of the Field is he who watches what takes place within this body.

Recognize me as the Knower of the Field in every body. I regard discrimination between Field and Knower as the highest kind of knowledge.

Now listen, and I will tell you briefly what the Field is; its nature, modifications and origin. I will tell you also who the Knower is, and what are his powers.

The sages have expressed these truths variously, in many hymns, and in aphorisms on the nature of Brahman, subtly reasoned and convincing in their arguments.

> Briefly I name them:
> First, Prakriti
> Which is the cosmos
> In cause unseen
> And visible feature;

Intellect, ego;
Earth, water and ether,
Air and fire;
Man's ten organs
Of knowing and doing,
Man's mind also;
The five sense-objects—*
Sound in its essence,
Essence of aspect,
Essence of odour,
Of touch and of tasting;
Hate and desire,
And pain and pleasure;
Consciousness, lastly,
And resolution;
These, with their sum
Which is blent in the body:
These make the Field
With its limits and changes.

Therefore I tell you:
Be humble, be harmless,
Have no pretension,
Be upright, forbearing,
Serve your teacher
In true obedience,
Keeping the mind
And the body in cleanness,
Tranquil, steadfast,
Master of ego,
Standing apart
From the things of the senses,
Free from self;
Aware of the weakness
In mortal nature,

* See Appendix I, page 135.

Its bondage to birth,
Age, suffering, dying;
To nothing be slave,
Nor desire possession
Of man-child or wife,
Of home or of household;
Calmly encounter
The painful, the pleasant;
Adore me only
With heart undistracted;
Turn all your thought
Toward solitude, spurning
The noise of the crowd,
Its fruitless commotion;
Strive without ceasing
To know the Atman,
Seek this knowledge
And comprehend clearly
Why you should seek it:
Such, it is said,
Are the roots of true wisdom:
Ignorance, merely,
Is all that denies them.

Now I shall describe That which has to be known, in order that its knower may gain immortality. That Brahman is beginningless, transcendent, eternal. He is said to be equally beyond what is, and what is not.

Everywhere are His hands, eyes, feet; His heads and
    His faces:
This whole world is His ear; He exists, encompas-
    sing all things;
Doing the tasks of each sense, yet Himself devoid of
    the senses:
Standing apart, He sustains: He is free from the
    gunas but feels them.

He is within and without: He lives in the live and
the lifeless:
Subtle beyond mind's grasp; so near us, so utterly
distant:
Undivided, He seems to divide into objects and
creatures;
Sending creation forth from Himself, He upholds
and withdraws it;
Light of all lights, He abides beyond our ignorant
darkness;
Knowledge, the one thing real we may study or
know, the heart's dweller.

Now I have told you briefly what the Field is,
what knowledge is, and what is that one Reality
which must be known. When my devotee knows
these things, he becomes fit to reach union with me.

You must understand that both Prakriti and Brahman are without beginning. All evolution and all
the gunas proceed from Prakriti. From Prakriti the
evolution of body and senses is said to originate.
The sense of individuality in us is said to cause our
experience of pleasure and pain. The individual
self, which is Brahman mistakenly identified with
Prakriti, experiences the gunas which proceed from
Prakriti. It is born of pure or impure parents, according to that kind of guna to which it is most
attached.

The supreme Brahman in this body is also known
as the Witness. It makes all our actions possible,
and, as it were, sanctions them, experiencing all our
experiences. It is the infinite Being, the supreme
Atman. He who has experienced Brahman directly
and known it to be other than Prakriti and the
gunas, will not be reborn, no matter how he has
lived his life.

Some, whose hearts are purified, realize the Atman within themselves through contemplation. Some realize the Atman philosophically, by meditating upon its independence of Prakriti. Others realize it by following the yoga of right action. Others, who do not know these paths, worship God as their teachers have taught them. If these faithfully practise what they have learned, they also will pass beyond death's power.

> Know this, O Prince:
> Of things created
> All are come forth
> From the seeming union
> Of Field and Knower,
> Prakriti with Brahman.

> Who sees his Lord
> Within every creature,
> Deathlessly dwelling
> Amidst the mortal:
> That man sees truly.

> Thus ever aware
> Of the Omnipresent
> Always about him,
> He offers no outrage
> To his own Atman,
> Hides the face of God
> Beneath ego no longer:
> Therefore he reaches
> That bliss which is highest.

> Who sees all action
> Ever performed
> Alone by Prakriti,
> That man sees truly:
> The Atman is actless.

Who sees the separate
Lives of all creatures
United in Brahman
Brought forth from Brahman,
Himself finds Brahman.

Not subject to change
Is the infinite Atman,
Without beginning,
Beyond the gunas:
Therefore, O Prince,
Though It dwells in the body,
It acts not, nor feels
The fruits of our action.

For, like the ether,
Pervading all things,
Too subtle for taint,
This Atman also
Inhabits all bodies
But never is tainted.

By the single sun
This whole world is illumined:
By its one Knower
The Field is illumined.

Who thus perceives
With the eye of wisdom
In what manner the Field
Is distinct from its Knower,
How men are made free
From the toils of Prakriti:
His aim is accomplished,
He enters the Highest.

XIV. *The Three Gunas*

SRI KRISHNA:
Once more I shall teach you
That uttermost wisdom:
The sages who found it
Were all made perfect,
Escaping the bonds of the body.

In that wisdom they lived,
Made one with my holy nature:
Now they are not reborn
When a new age begins,
Nor have they any part
In its dissolution.

Prakriti, this vast womb,
I quicken into birth
With the seed of all life:
Thence, O son of Bharata,
The many creatures spring.

Many are the forms of the living,
Many the wombs that bear them;
Prakriti, the womb of all wombs
And I the seed-giving Father.

From Prakriti the gunas come forth,
Sattwa, rajas, tamas:
These are the bonds that bind
The undying dweller
Imprisoned in the body.

Sattwa the shining
Can show the Atman
By its pure light:
Yet sattwa will bind you
To search for happiness,
Longing for knowledge.

Rajas the passionate
Will make you thirsty
For pleasure and possession:
Rajas will bind you
To hunger for action.

Tamas the ignorant
Bewilders all men:
Tamas will bind you
With bonds of delusion,
Sluggishness, stupor.

The power of sattwa
Enslaves the happy,
The power of rajas
Enslaves the doers,
The power of tamas
Enslaves the deluded
And darkens their judgment.

When sattwa prevails
Over rajas, tamas,
Man feels that sattwa:
When rajas prevails
Over sattwa, tamas,
Man is seized by that rajas:
When tamas prevails
Over rajas, sattwa,
Man yields to that tamas.

When understanding
Shines in through the senses,
The doors of the body:
Know sattwa is present.
In greed, in the heat of action,
In eager enterprise,
In restlessness, in all desire,
Know rajas the ruler.

When the mind is dark,
Bewildered, slothful
And lost in delusion:
Know tamas prevailing.

That man who meets death
In the hour of sattwa
Goes to a sinless home
Among the saints of God.

He who dies in rajas
Will be reborn
Among those whose bondage is action:
He who dies in tamas will return
To the womb of a dullard.

Fruit of the righteous act
Is sattwa, purest joy:
As for the deeds of rajas,
Pain is their fruit:
Truly, ignorance is all
The fruit of tamas.

Of sattwa, knowledge is born;
Of rajas, greed;
Tamas brings forth bewilderment,
Delusion, darkness.

> Abiding in sattwa,
> Man goes to higher realms;
> Remaining in rajas,
> In this world he remains;
> Sunk in tamas,
> His lowest nature,
> He sinks to the underworld.
>
> Let the wise man know
> These gunas alone as the doers
> Of every action;
> Let him learn to know That
> Which is beyond them, also:
> Thus he will reach my oneness.
>
> When the dweller in the body
> Has overcome the gunas
> That cause this body,
> Then he is made free
> From birth and death,
> From pain and decay:
> He becomes immortal.

A man is said to have transcended the gunas when he does not hate the light of sattwa, or the activity of rajas, or even the delusion of tamas, while these prevail; and yet does not long for them after they have ceased. He is like one who sits unconcerned, and is not disturbed by the gunas. He knows that they are the doers of all action, and never loses this power of discrimination. He rests in the inner calm of the Atman, regarding happiness and suffering as one. Gold, mud and stone are of equal value to him. The pleasant and the unpleasant are alike. He has true discernment. He pays no attention to praise or to blame. His behaviour is the same

when he is honoured and when he is insulted. When
men go to war, he does not regard either side as his
enemies or his partisans. He feels no lack of anything; therefore he never initiates any action.

He who worships me with unfaltering love transcends these gunas. He becomes fit to reach union
with Brahman.

> For I am Brahman
> Within this body,
> Life immortal
> That shall not perish:
> I am the Truth
> And the Joy for ever.

XV. Devotion To the Supreme Spirit

SRI KRISHNA:

> There is a fig tree
> In ancient story,
> The giant Aswattha,
> The everlasting,
> Rooted in heaven,
> Its branches earthward:
> Each of its leaves
> Is a song of the Vedas,
> And he who knows it
> Knows all the Vedas.

> Downward and upward
> Its branches bending
> Are fed by the gunas,
> The buds it puts forth
> Are the things of the senses,

Roots it has also
Reaching downward
Into this world,
The roots of man's action.

What its form is,
Its end and beginning,
Its very nature,
Can never be known here.

Therefore, a man should contemplate Brahman until he has sharpened the axe of his non-attachment. With this axe, he must cut through the firmly-rooted Aswattha tree. Then he must try to realize that state from which there is no return to future births. Let him take refuge in that Primal Being, from whom all this seeming activity streams forth for ever.

When men have thrown off their ignorance, they are free from pride and delusion. They have conquered the evil of worldly attachment. They live in constant union with the Atman. All craving has left them. They are no longer at the mercy of opposing sense-reactions. Thus they reach that state which is beyond all change.

This is my Infinite Being; shall the sun lend it
Any light—or the moon, or fire? For it shines
Self-luminous always: and he who attains me
Will never be reborn.

Part of myself is the God within every creature,
Keeps that nature eternal, yet seems to be separate,
Putting on mind and senses five, the garment
Made of Prakriti.

When the Lord puts on a body, or casts it from him,
He enters or departs, taking the mind and senses
Away with him, as the wind steals perfume
Out of the flowers.

Watching over the ear and the eye, and presiding
There behind touch, and taste, and smell, he is also
Within the mind: he enjoys and suffers
The things of the senses.

Dwelling in flesh, or departing, or one with the
      gunas,
Knowing their moods and motions, he is invisible
Always to the ignorant, but his sages see him
With the eye of wisdom.

Yogis who have gained tranquillity through the
practice of spiritual disciplines, behold him in their
own consciousness. But those who lack tranquillity
and discernment will not find him, even though they
may try hard to do so.

The light that lives in the sun,
Lighting all the world,
The light of the moon,
The light that is in fire:
Know that light to be mine.

My energy enters the earth,
Sustaining all that lives:
I become the moon,
Giver of water and sap,
To feed the plants and the trees.

Flame of life in all,
I consume the many foods,
Turning them into strength
That upholds the body.

I am in all hearts,
I give and take away
Knowledge and memory:
I am all that the Vedas tell,
I am the teacher,
The knower of Vedanta.

There are two kinds of personality in this world,
the mortal and the immortal. The personality of all
creatures is mortal. The personality of God is said to
be immortal. It is the same for ever. But there is
one other than these; the Impersonal Being who is
called the supreme Atman. He is the unchanging
Lord who pervades and supports the three worlds.
And since I, the Atman, transcend the mortal and
even the immortal, I am known in this world and in
the Vedas as the supreme Reality.

He who is free from delusion, and knows me as
the supreme Reality, knows all that can be known.
Therefore he adores me with his whole heart.

This is the most sacred of all the truths I have
taught you. He who has realized it becomes truly
wise. The purpose of his life is fulfilled.

XVI. Divine and Demonic Tendencies

A man who is born with tendencies toward the Divine, is fearless and pure in heart. He perseveres in that path to union with Brahman which the scriptures and his teacher have taught him. He is charitable. He can control his passions. He studies the scriptures regularly, and obeys their directions. He practises spiritual disciplines. He is straightforward, truthful, and of an even temper. He harms no one. He renounces the things of this world. He has a tranquil mind and an unmalicious tongue. He is compassionate toward all. He is not greedy. He is gentle and modest. He abstains from useless activity. He has faith in the strength of his higher nature. He can forgive and endure. He is clean in thought and act. He is free from hatred and from pride. Such qualities are his birthright.

When a man is born with demonic tendencies, his birthright is hypocrisy, arrogance, conceit, anger, cruelty and ignorance.

The birthright of the divine nature leads to liberation. The birthright of the demonic nature leads to greater bondage. But you need not fear, Arjuna: your birthright is divine.

In this world there are two kinds of beings: those whose nature tends toward the Divine, and those who have the demonic tendencies. I have already described the divine nature to you in some detail. Now you shall learn more about the demonic nature.

Men of demonic nature know neither what they

114

ought to do, nor what they should refrain from doing. There is no truth in them, or purity, or right conduct. They maintain that the scriptures are a lie, and that the universe is not based upon a moral law, but godless, conceived in lust and created by copulation, without any other cause. Because they believe this in the darkness of their little minds, these degraded creatures do horrible deeds, attempting to destroy the world. They are enemies of mankind.

Their lust can never be appeased. They are arrogant, and vain, and drunk with pride. They run blindly after what is evil. The ends they work for are unclean. They are sure that life has only one purpose: gratification of the senses. And so they are plagued by innumerable cares, from which death alone can release them. Anxiety binds them with a hundred chains, delivering them over to lust and wrath. They are ceaselessly busy, piling up dishonest gains to satisfy their cravings.

'I wanted this and to-day I got it. I want that: I shall get it to-morrow. All these riches are now mine: soon I shall have more. I have killed this enemy. I will kill all the rest. I am a ruler of men. I enjoy the things of this world. I am successful, strong and happy. Who is my equal? I am so wealthy and so nobly born. I will sacrifice to the gods. I will give alms. I will make merry.' That is what they say to themselves, in the blindness of their ignorance.

They are addicts of sensual pleasure, made restless by their many desires, and caught in the net of delusion. They fall into the filthy hell of their own evil minds. Conceited, haughty, foolishly proud, and intoxicated by their wealth, they offer sacrifice to God in name only, for outward show, without following the sacred rituals. These malignant creatures are full of egoism, vanity, lust, wrath, and conscious-ness of power. They loathe me, and deny my pres-ence both in themselves and in others. They are enemies of all men and of myself; cruel, despicable and vile. I cast them back, again and again, into the wombs of degraded parents, subjecting them to the wheel of birth and death. And so they are con-stantly reborn, in degradation and delusion. They do not reach me, but sink down to the lowest possible condition of the soul.

Hell has three doors: lust, rage and greed. These lead to man's ruin. Therefore he must avoid them all. He who passes by these three dark doors has achieved his own salvation. He will reach the high-est goal at last.

But he who flouts the commandments of the scrip-tures, and acts on the impulse of his desires, cannot reach perfection, or happiness, or the highest goal.

Let the scriptures be your guide, therefore, in de-ciding what you must do, and what you must abstain from. First learn the path of action, as the scriptures teach it. Then act accordingly.

XVII. Three Kinds of Faith

ARJUNA:

There are men who sacrifice to God with faith in their hearts, although they do not follow the instruc-tions of the scriptures. What is the nature of that faith? Does it belong to sattwa, or to rajas, or to tamas?

SRI KRISHNA:

Faith, among human beings, is of three kinds. It is characterized by sattwa, or by rajas, or by tamas, according to a man's dominant tendencies. Now listen. The faith of each individual corresponds to his temperament. A man consists of the faith that is in him. Whatever his faith is, he is.

Men whose temperament is dominated by sattwa, worship God, in His various aspects. Men of rajas worship power and wealth. As for the rest—the men of tamas—they worship the spirits of the dead, and make gods of the ghosts of their ancestors.

You may know these men to be of demonic nature who mortify the body excessively, in ways not prescribed by the scriptures. They do this because their lust and attachment to sense-objects has filled them with egotism and vanity. In their foolishness, they weaken all their sense-organs, and outrage me, the dweller within the body.

The food which is agreeable to different men is also of three sorts. So, too, are the kinds of sacrifice, austerity and alms-giving. Listen; this is how they may be distinguished.

Men of sattwa like foods which increase their vital force, energy, strength and health. Such foods add to the pleasure of physical and mental life. They are juicy, soothing, fresh and agreeable. But men of rajas prefer foods which are violently bitter, sour, salty, hot, pungent, acid and burning. These cause ill-health, and distemper of the mind and body. And men of tamas take a perverse pleasure in foods which are stale, tasteless, rotten and impure. They like to eat the leavings of others.

When men offer sacrifice in accordance with scriptural instructions, and do not desire any advan-

tage for themselves, they are inspired by sattwa.
Their hearts are set upon the sacrifice, for its own
sake. An inner sense of duty impels them. But you
may be sure that the performance of sacrifice for
outward show, and in the hope of divine reward,
is inspired by rajas. When the givers of the sacrifice are inspired by tamas, they disregard the scriptural instructions: there is no food-offering, no
prayer of dedication, no gift to the chief priest, and
no faith at all.

Reverence for the devas, the seers, the teachers
and the sages; straightforwardness, harmlessness,
physical cleanliness and sexual purity; these are the
virtues whose practice is called austerity of the
body. To speak without ever causing pain to another, to be truthful, to say always what is kind and
beneficial, and to study the scriptures regularly:
this practice is called austerity of speech. The practice of serenity, sympathy, meditation upon the Atman, withdrawal of the mind from sense-objects,
and integrity of motive, is called austerity of the
mind. When men practise this threefold austerity
devotedly, with enlightened faith and no desire for
reward, it is said to have the nature of sattwa.

Austerity which is practised out of selfish pride,
or to gain notoriety, honour and worship, is said to
have the nature of rajas. Its effect is not lasting,
because it lacks resolution. Austerity is said to have
the nature of tamas when it is practised for some
foolish purpose, or for the excitement of self-torture,
or in order to harm another person.*

A gift may be regarded as proceeding from sattwa
when it is given to a deserving person, at a suitable
time, and in a fit place; not because of past bene-
fits, or in the hope of a future reward, but simply
because the giver knows that it is right for him to

* i.e. 'Black Magic.'

give. Whatever is given in the hope of a like return, or with any other selfish motive, or reluctantly, may be known to proceed from rajas. From tamas comes the gift which is given to an unworthy person, at the wrong time and in the wrong place, disdainfully, without regard for the feelings of him who receives it.

OM TAT SAT: these three words designate Brahman, by whom the seers, the Vedas and the sacrificial rites were created in ancient times. Therefore OM is always uttered by the devotees of Brahman, as the scriptures direct, before undertaking any act of sacrifice, almsgiving or austerity. TAT, meaning the Absolute, is uttered by seekers after liberation who desire no reward for their deed, when they are about to make sacrifice, or give alms, or practise some austerity. SAT means goodness, and existence. It also means an auspicious act. All perseverance in sacrifice, austerity or almsgiving is SAT. All actions dedicated to Brahman are SAT.

If a man performs any act of sacrifice, or gives any gift, or practises any austerity without directing his faith and will toward Brahman, then what he does is *asat*, unreal. It cannot produce any good result, either in this world or the next.

XVIII. The Yoga of Renunciation

ARJUNA:

I want to learn the truth about renunciation and non-attachment. What is the difference between these two principles?

SRI KRISHNA:

The sages tell us that renunciation means the complete giving-up of all actions which are motivated by desire. And they say that non-attachment means abandonment of the fruits of action.

Some philosophers declare that all kinds of action should be given up, because action always contains a certain measure of evil. Others say that acts of sacrifice, almsgiving and austerity should not be given up. Now you shall hear the truth of this matter.

Acts of sacrifice, almsgiving and austerity should not be given up: their performance is necessary. For sacrifice, almsgiving and austerity are a means of purification to those who rightly understand them. But even these acts must be performed without attachment or regard for their fruits. Such is my final and considered judgment.

Renunciation is said to be of three kinds. If a man, in his ignorance, renounces those actions which the scriptures ordain, his renunciation is inspired by tamas. If he abstains from any action merely because it is disagreeable, or because he fears it will cause him bodily pain, his renunciation is inspired by rajas. He will not obtain any spiritual benefit from such renunciation. But when a man performs an action which is sanctioned by the scriptures, and does it for duty's sake only, renouncing all attachment and desire for its fruits, then his renunciation is inspired by sattwa.

When a man is endowed with spiritual discrimination and illumined by knowledge of the Atman, all his doubts are dispelled. He does not shrink from doing what is disagreeable to him, nor does he long to do what is agreeable. No human being can give up action altogether, but he who gives up the fruits of action is said to be non-attached.

To those who have not yet renounced the ego and its desires, action bears three kinds of fruit—pleasant, unpleasant, and a mixture of both. They will be reaped in due season. But those who have renounced ego and desire will reap no fruit at all, either in this world or in the next.

> All our action
> Has five partakers:
> So say the scriptures
> That teach us wisdom
> To break the bondage
> Earned by our action:
> Listen and learn them.

> First, this body;
> Then ego, the doer;
> The organs of sense
> And the many motions
> Of Life in the body;
> Lastly, the devas
> In spirit presiding.*

> Whatever the action,
> Excellent, evil;
> Whether of speech,
> Of mind, or of body:
> These are its causers.

> Falsely he sees,
> And with small discernment,
> Who sees this Atman
> The doer of action:
> His mind is not purged
> In the work of the spirit.

* According to Hindu mythology, each sense-organ has a presiding deity.

But he whose mind dwells
Beyond attachment,
Untainted by ego,
No act shall bind him
With any bond:
Though he slay these thousands
He is no slayer.

There are three things which motivate action:
knowledge, the knower and that which is known.
There are three constituents of action: the instrument, the purpose and the doer. Sankhya* philosophy declares that knowledge, action and doer are of
three kinds only, according to the guna which predominates in each. Listen, this is their nature.

There is that knowledge
From sattwa proceeding
Which knows one Being
Deathless in every creature,
Entire amidst all division.

The knowledge that is rajas
Knows nothing but difference:
Many souls in many creatures,
All various, each
Apart from his fellow.

The knowledge that is tamas
Knows no reason:
Its sight distorted
Takes the part for the whole,
Misreading Nature.

* The system of philosophy compiled by Kapila.

The act of sacred duty,
Done without attachment,
Not as pleasure desired,
Not as hated compulsion,
By him who has no care
For the fruit of his action:
That act is of sattwa.

The act of weary toil
Done in despite of nature
Under the whip of lust
And the will of the ego:
That act is of rajas.

The act undertaken
In the hour of delusion
Without count of cost,
Squandering strength and treasure,
Heedless of harm to another,
By him who does not question
His power to perform it:
That act is of tamas.

The doer without desire,
Who does not boast of his deed,
Who is ardent, enduring,
Untouched by triumph,
In failure untroubled:
He is a man of sattwa.

The doer with desire,
Hot for the prize of vainglory,
Brutal, greedy and foul,
In triumph too quick to rejoice,
In failure despairing:
He is a man of rajas.

The indifferent doer
Whose heart is not in his deed,
Stupid and stubborn,
A cheat, and malicious,
The idle lover of delay,
Easily dejected:
He is a man of tamas.

There are three kinds of conscience and three kinds of determination, according to the predominance of each guna. Now listen: I will explain them fully, one by one.

A man's conscience has the nature of sattwa when it can distinguish between the paths of renunciation and worldly desire. Then it knows what actions are right or wrong, what is safe and what is dangerous, what binds the embodied spirit and what sets it free. But when the conscience cannot distinguish truly between right and wrong, or know what should and what should not be done, then it has the nature of rajas. And when the conscience is so thickly wrapped in ignorance that it mistakes wrong for right and sees everything distorted, then it has the nature of tamas.

Determination inspired by sattwa never wavers. It is strengthened by the practice of yoga. A man who has this kind of determination gains absolute control over his mind, vital energy and senses. Rajas, on the other hand, inspires that kind of determination with which a man follows the object of his desire, or seeks wealth, or does a duty, looking for reward and personal advantage. As for the determination inspired by tamas, it is nothing but obstinacy. It makes a man stubbornly refuse to shake off his dullness, fear, grief, low spirits or vanity.

And now, Arjuna, I will tell you about the three kinds of happiness:

Who knows the Atman
Knows that happiness
Born of pure knowledge:
The joy of sattwa.
Deep his delight
After strict self-schooling:
Sour toil at first
But at last what sweetness,
The end of sorrow.

Senses also
Have joy in their marriage
With things of the senses,
Sweet at first
But at last how bitter:
Steeped in rajas,
That pleasure is poison.
Bred of tamas
Is brutish contentment
In stupor and sloth
And obstinate error:
Its end, its beginning
Alike are delusion.

There is no creature, either on earth or among
the devas in heaven, who is free from these three
gunas which come forth from Prakriti.

Seer and leader,
Provider and server:*
Each has the duty
Ordained by his nature
Born of the gunas.

* See note on Chapter IX, page 85.

The seer's duty,
Ordained by his nature,
Is to be tranquil
In mind and in spirit,
Self-controlled,
Austere and stainless,
Upright, forbearing;
To follow wisdom,
To know the Atman,
Firm of faith
In the truth that is Brahman.

The leader's duty,
Ordained by his nature,
Is to be bold,
Unflinching and fearless,
Subtle of skill
And open-handed,
Great-hearted in battle,
A resolute ruler.

Others are born
To the tasks of providing:
These are the traders,
The cultivators,
The breeders of cattle.

To work for all men,
Such is the duty
Ordained for the servers:
This is their nature.
All mankind
Is born for perfection
And each shall attain it
Will he but follow
His nature's duty.

Now you shall hear how a man may become perfect, if he devotes himself to the work which is natural to him. A man will reach perfection if he does his duty as an act of worship to the Lord, who is the source of the universe, prompting all action, everywhere present.

A man's own natural duty, even if it seems imperfectly done, is better than work not naturally his own even if this is well performed. When a man acts according to the law of his nature, he cannot be sinning. Therefore, no one should give up his natural work, even though he does it imperfectly. For all action is involved in imperfection, like fire in smoke.

When a man has achieved non-attachment, self-mastery and freedom from desire through renunciation, he reaches union with Brahman, who is beyond all action.

Learn from me now,
O son of Kunti,
How man made perfect
Is one with Brahman,
The goal of wisdom.
When the mind and the heart
Are freed from delusion,
United with Brahman,
When steady will
Has subdued the senses,
When sight and taste
And sound are abandoned
Without regretting,
Without aversion;
When man seeks solitude,
Eats but little,
Curbing his speech,
His mind and his body,

Ever engaged
In his meditation
On Brahman the truth,
And full of compassion;
When he casts from him
Vanity, violence,
Pride, lust, anger
And all his possessions,
Totally free
From the sense of ego
And tranquil of heart:
That man is ready
For oneness with Brahman.
And he who dwells
United with Brahman,
Calm in mind,
Not grieving, not craving,
Regarding all men
With equal acceptance:
He loves me most dearly.

To love is to know me,
My innermost nature,
The truth that I am:
Through this knowledge he enters
At once to my Being.

All that he does
Is offered before me
In utter surrender:
My grace is upon him,
He finds the eternal,
The place unchanging.

Mentally resign all your action to me. Regard me
as your dearest loved one. Know me to be your only
refuge. Be united always in heart and consciousness
with me.

United with me, you shall overcome all difficulties by my grace. But if your heart is full of conceit, and you do not heed me, you are lost. If, in your vanity, you say: 'I will not fight,' your resolve is vain. Your own nature will drive you to the act. For you yourself have created the karma that binds you. You are helpless in its power. And you will do that very thing which your ignorance seeks to avoid.

The Lord lives in the heart of every creature. He turns them round and round upon the wheel of his Maya. Take refuge utterly in him. By his grace you will find supreme peace, and the state which is beyond all change.

Now I have taught you that wisdom which is the secret of secrets. Ponder it carefully. Then act as you think best. These are the last words that I shall say to you, the deepest of all truths. I speak for your own good. You are the friend I chose and love.

> Give me your whole heart,
> Love and adore me,
> Worship me always,
> Bow to me only,
> And you shall find me:
> This is my promise
> Who love you dearly.

> Lay down all duties
> In me, your refuge.
> Fear no longer,
> For I will save you
> From sin and from bondage.

You must never tell this holy truth to anyone who lacks self-control and devotion, or who despises his teacher and mocks at me. But the man who loves me, and teaches my devotees this supreme truth of the Gita, will certainly come to me. No one can do me a higher service than this. No one on earth can be dearer to me.

And if any man meditates upon this sacred discourse of ours, I shall consider that he has worshipped me in spirit. Even if a man simply listens to these words with faith, and does not doubt them, he will be freed from his sins and reach the heaven of the righteous.

Have you listened carefully, Arjuna, to everything I have told you? Have I dispelled the delusions of your ignorance?

ARJUNA:

By your grace, O Lord, my delusions have been dispelled. My mind stands firm. Its doubts are ended. I will do your bidding.

SANJAYA:

Such were the words that thrilled my heart, that marvellous discourse,

Heard from the lips of the high-souled Prince and the great Lord Krishna,

Not with these earthly ears, but by mystic grace of Vyasa,

Thus I learned that yoga supreme from the Master of yogis.

Ever and ever again I rejoice, O King, and remember

Sacred and wonderful truths that Krishna told to his comrade.

Ever again, O King, I am glad and remember rejoicing

That most splendid of forms put on by Krishna, the Sweet One.

Where Lord Krishna is, and Arjuna, great among archers,

There, I know, is goodness and peace, and triumph and glory.

OM. Peace. Peace. Peace.

The Cosmology of the Gita

LIKE ALL OTHER WORKS of Hindu religious literature, the Gita is based upon a clearly-defined system of cosmology. The single, central fact of this cosmology is called Brahman, the Reality. Brahman is the total Godhead. It can never be defined or expressed. The Upanishads say that Brahman is Existence, Knowledge and Bliss; but these are not attributes. Brahman cannot be said to exist. Brahman is Existence itself. Brahman is not wise or happy, but absolute Knowledge, absolute Joy. Another method of approach, more acceptable perhaps to our human minds, is to say: 'Brahman is not this, Brahman is not that . . .' until the entire phenomenal universe has been eliminated, and Brahman alone remains.

Being absolutely present, Brahman is within all creatures and objects. The Godhead is present in man, in the mouse, in the stone, in the flash of lightning. Thus considered, Brahman is called the At-man—a term of convenience merely, which does not imply the slightest difference. The Atman and Brahman are one.

Again, when Brahman is considered in relation to this universe, He is regarded as a personal God, Ishwara. Ishwara is God with attributes. He contains all the divine qualities of love, mercy, purity, justice, knowledge and truth.

Brahman, being the Absolute, is beyond all action. Therefore Brahman cannot be said to create or to destroy. It is Ishwara, Brahman united with His power, who creates this universe, preserves it and dissolves it. To say this is not necessarily to imply

a dualism. Brahman's power can no more be separated from Brahman than the heat of fire can be
separated from fire itself. But philosophical analysis
cannot take us any further into this tremendous
mystery. The conception of Ishwara represents all
that the human intellect can know of God. Brahman,
in the absolute sense, cannot possibly be known by
the conscious mind. Brahman can only be experienced in that superconscious state achieved by the
saints, which is called samadhi, or union with God.
The methods of reaching this state are described
at length in the Bhagavad-Gita. When all sense-
contact with the outer world has been broken, by
means of discrimination, spiritual discipline and
meditation, the mind is able to turn inward upon
itself and realize the presence of the Atman, the
immanent Godhead. This is the technique of all
mystical practice, and it has been taught by every
true religion.

Hinduism has further personified the three functions or aspects of Ishwara as Brahma, Vishnu and
Shiva. Brahma represents the divine function of creation, Vishnu preservation, and Shiva dissolution.
Shiva is often spoken of as 'the destroyer,' but this
is a misleading word, because the universe is never
destroyed. Since it is subject to the eternal power of
Brahman, the universe is part of a beginningless and
endless process, which alternates between the two
phases of potentiality and expression. When, at the
end of a time-cycle, or kalpa, the universe is dissolved, it passes into a phase of potentiality, a seed-
state, and thus awaits its next creation. In Chapter
VIII of the Gita, this process is described. The phase
of expression is called by Sri Krishna 'the day of
Brahma,' and the phase of potentiality 'the night of
Brahma.' The creatures inhabiting the worlds subject to these cycles are perpetually being reborn and

redissolved, with each succeeding cosmic day and night. This dissolution should not, however, be thought of as 'going back to God.' The creature merely returns to the power of Brahman which sent it forth, and remains there in an unmanifested state, until the time comes for its re-manifestation.

The power of Brahman is the basis of all mind and matter. It is called Prakriti, or Maya: the terms are interchangeable. According to the Gita, Ishwara makes Himself a body out of Prakriti whenever He chooses to be born among men. Nevertheless, because He is God, He remains master of Prakriti even in His human form. It is in this that the divine incarnation differs from the ordinary mortal. Man, also, is the Atman associated with Prakriti, or Maya. But man is subject to Prakriti, and deluded by It into thinking that he is not the Atman. To become united with the Atman is to throw off this delusion, and to win liberation from the process of birth and death. The liberated man cannot be reborn, because he is no longer subject to the power of Prakriti. The divine incarnation is never subject to this power: he enters the universe and leaves it at will.

Hinduism accepts the belief in many divine incarnations, including Krishna, Buddha and Jesus, and foresees that there will be many more:

> In every age I come back
> To deliver the holy,
> To destroy the sin of the sinner,
> To establish righteousness.

Prakriti is said to be composed of three forces, known as the gunas. They are sattwa, rajas and tamas. During the 'night of Brahma,' the phase of potentiality, these gunas are in a state of perfect equilibrium, and Prakriti remains undifferentiated.

Creation is the disturbance of this equilibrium. The gunas then begin to enter into a vast variety of combinations, corresponding to the various forms of differentiated mind and matter. Their characteristics may be known from their products in the psychic and physical worlds.

In the physical world, sattwa embodies all that is pure and fine, rajas embodies the active principle, and tamas the principle of solidity and resistance. All three are present in everything, but one guna always predominates. For example, sattwa predominates in sunlight, rajas in an erupting volcano, and tamas in a block of granite.

The gunas also represent the different stages in the evolution in any particular entity. Sattwa is the essence of the form to be realized; tamas is the inherent obstacle to its realization; and rajas is the power by which that obstacle is removed and the essential form becomes manifest.

In the mind of man, sattwa expresses itself psychologically as tranquillity, purity and calmness; rajas as passion, restlessness, aggressive activity; tamas as stupidity, laziness, inertia. Sometimes one guna is predominant, sometimes another; and a man's mood and character vary accordingly. But man can cultivate any one of the gunas, by his actions and thoughts and way of living. We are taught that tamas can be overcome by the cultivation of rajas, and rajas by the cultivation of sattwa. However, the ultimate ideal is to transcend sattwa also and reach the Atman, which is above and beyond the gunas.

In tracing the evolution of differentiated matter from Prakriti, we begin with mahat, the basis of the individual intelligence. Next comes buddhi, the faculty by which objects are distinguished and classified. Then ahamkara, the ego-sense. Ahamkara divides itself into three functions: (1) manas, which receives impressions from the senses and carries them to buddhi; (2) the five organs of perception—sight, smell, hearing, taste and touch—and the five organs of action—tongue, feet, hands, and the organs of evacuation and reproduction—and (3) the five tanmatras, the essences of sound, touch, aspect, taste and smell. These subtle tanmatras, combining and recombining, produce the five gross elements, earth, water, fire, air and ether, of which the external universe is composed.

The whole system may be shown diagrammatically, as seen below.

PRAKRITI

MAHAT

BUDDHI

AHAMKARA

Five Organs of Perception
Five Organs of Action

Manas   Five Tanmatras

Five Gross Elements

We must beware of trying to force the hypotheses of modern western Science into the frame of the Hindu world-picture. Yet certain points of agreement exist between them, and should not be disregarded.

Modern Science has, of course, no concern with the concept of Absolute Reality. It does not seek to know Brahman. Nor does it offer confirmation of the validity of the mystic's claim to superconsciousness. It says, in effect: 'For the present, at any rate, we have no technique for investigating this type of experience. When you speak of knowing Brahman you are speaking in extra-scientific terms.'

Nevertheless, if we consider Prakriti and the gunas, we find that Science and Vedanta are talking the same language. Science, also, postulates a monistic universe. All matter is made up of different combinations of the chemical elements; and these elements are composed of combinations of identical units. Man is all of a piece with this world and with the most distant of the stars.

Science makes no basic distinction between mind and matter. Mind is everywhere potential. If the scientist cannot yet detect mind in a stone, he believes that this is only because he lacks a suitable method of doing so. He finds no point in evolution at which life can be said to enter, no point at which personality suddenly invests the fœtus or the growing infant. Evolution, he tells us, is perfectly continuous, and it has a general direction.

Man's ideals and values are relative, perpetually evolving. The goal is not known, but its direction is apparent, and it is Man's evolutionary mission to move continually toward it, as Columbus sailed toward the unknown West. From the scientific point of view, Man's mission is to acquire greater and greater knowledge of his relation to his environment, and to gain increasing control over it, since it is really part of himself. And so Arjuna and the scientist are both asking the same question: 'What am I?'

The Gita and War

BEFORE THE BATTLE of Kurukshetra begins, Arjuna asks Krishna to drive their chariot into the open space between the two armies, so that he may see the men he must fight with. When Krishna does this, Arjuna recognizes many of his kinsmen and old friends among the ranks of the enemy. He is appalled by the realization that he is about to kill those whom he loves better than life itself. In his despair, he exclaims: 'I will not fight!'

Krishna's reply to Arjuna occupies the rest of the book. It deals not only with Arjuna's immediate personal problem, but with the whole nature of action, the meaning of life, and the aims for which man must struggle, here on earth. At the end of their conversation, Arjuna has changed his mind. He is ready to fight. And the battle begins.

To understand the Gita, we must first consider what it is and what it is not. We must consider its setting. When Jesus spoke the words which are recorded as the Sermon on the Mount, he was addressing a group of dedicated followers, in a peaceful country atmosphere, far from strife and confusion. And so he taught them the highest and strictest ideal, the ideal of non-violence. The Gita is very different. Krishna and Arjuna are on a battlefield.

Arjuna is not a dedicated monk but a householder
and a warrior by birth and profession. He corresponds to the medieval knight of Christendom. His
problem is considered in relation to the circumstances of the moment.

In teaching Arjuna, Krishna employs two sets of
values, the relative and the absolute. He begins by
dealing with Arjuna's feelings of revulsion, on general grounds. Arjuna shrinks from the act of killing.
Krishna reminds him that, in the absolute sense,
there is no such act. The Atman, the indwelling
Godhead, is the only reality. This body is simply
an appearance; its existence, its destruction, are
alike illusory. Having said this, Krishna goes on to
discuss Arjuna's individual problem. For Arjuna, a
member of the warrior caste, the fighting of this
battle is undoubtedly 'righteous.' His cause is just.
To defend it is his duty. In the Gita, we find that
the caste system is presented as a natural order.
Men are divided into four groups, according to their
capacities and characteristics. Each group has its
peculiar duties, ethics and responsibilities; and
these must be accepted. It is the way of spiritual
growth. A man must go forward from where he
stands. He cannot jump to the absolute; he must
evolve toward it. He cannot arbitrarily assume the
duties which belong to another group. 'Prefer to
die doing your own duty,' Krishna teaches. 'The
duty of another will bring you into great spiritual
danger.' Socially, the caste system is graded; but,
spiritually, there are no such distinctions. Everyone,
says Krishna, can attain the highest sainthood by
following the prescribed path of his own caste duty.
And in Europe, as in Asia, there have been men
who grew into spiritual giants while carrying out
their duties as merchants, peasants, doctors, popes,
scullions, or kings.

In the purely physical sphere of action, Arjuna is, indeed, no longer a free agent. The act of war is upon him; it has evolved out of his previous actions. At any given moment in time, we are what we are; and we have to accept the consequences of being ourselves. Only through this acceptance can we begin to evolve further. We may select the battle-ground. We cannot avoid the battle.

Arjuna is bound to act, but he is still free to make his choice between two different ways of performing the action. In general, mankind almost always acts with attachment; that is to say, with fear and desire. Desire for a certain result and fear that this result will not be obtained. Attached action binds us to the world of appearances; to the continual doing of more action. But there is another way of performing action, and this is without fear and without desire. The Christians call it 'holy indifference' and the Hindus 'non-attachment.' Both names are slightly misleading. They suggest coldness and lack of enthusiasm. That is why people often confuse non-attachment with fatalism, when, actually, they are opposites. The fatalist simply does not care. He will get what is coming to him. Why make any effort? But the doer of non-attached action is the most conscientious of men. Freed from fear and desire, he offers everything he does as a sacrament of devotion to his duty. All work becomes equally and vitally important. It is only toward the results of work—success or failure, praise or blame—that he remains indifferent. When action is done in this spirit, Krishna teaches, it will lead us to the knowledge of what is behind action, behind all life: the ultimate Reality. And, with the growth of this knowledge, the need for further action will gradually fall away from us. We shall realize our true nature, which is God.

It follows, therefore, that every action, under certain circumstances and for certain people, may be a stepping-stone to spiritual growth—if it is done in the spirit of non-attachment. All good and all evil is relative to the individual point of growth. For each individual, certain acts are absolutely wrong. Indeed, there may well be acts which are absolutely wrong for every individual alive on earth to-day. But, in the highest sense, there can be neither good nor evil. Because Krishna is speaking as God himself, he can take this attitude, and advise Arjuna to fight. There is no question, here, of doing evil that good may come. The Gita does not countenance such opportunism. Arjuna is to do the best he knows, in order to pass beyond that best to better. Later, his fighting at Kurukshetra may seem evil to him, and it *will* be evil—then. Doing the evil you know to be evil will never bring good. It will lead only to more evil, more attachment, more ignorance.

The Gita is sometimes accused of sanctioning war, and of being thus in opposition to the teachings of Christ, Buddha, and other great spiritual masters. In fact, the Gita neither sanctions war nor condemns it. Regarding no action as of absolute value, either for good or for evil, it cannot possibly do either. Its message should warn us not to dare to judge others. How can we prescribe our neighbour's duty when it is so hard for us to know our own? The pacifist must respect Arjuna. Arjuna must respect the pacifist. Both are going toward the same goal, if they are really sincere. There is an underlying solidarity between them which can be expressed, if each one follows, without compromise, the path upon which he finds himself. For we can only help others to do their duty by doing what we ourselves believe to be right. It is the one supremely social act.

Readers of the BHAGAVAD-GITA will be interested in an account of its influence on one of the great men of our time. This excerpt is from the fascinating new biography,

GANDHI-*His Life and Message for the World*
by
LOUIS FISCHER

A Signet Key book published by the New American Library of World Literature, Inc.

Mahatma Gandhi and the Bhagavad-Gita
by
LOUIS FISCHER

"RESIST NOT EVIL, but whosoever shall smite thee on thy right cheek, turn to him the left also . . . Blessed are the meek . . . Blessed are ye when men shall revile you and persecute you . . . Agree with thine adversary quickly . . . Forgive men their trespasses . . . Lay not up for yourself treasure upon earth . . . for where your treasure is, there will your heart be also . . ." These words of Christ "delighted" Mahatma Gandhi. They reminded him of the *Bhagavad-Gita,* the sacred book of the Hindus, which, he admitted to his shame, he had not read until his second year as a law student in London. It produced a tremendous impact which remained throughout life. "When doubts haunt me, when disappointments stare me in the face, and I see not one ray of hope on the horizon," he wrote in his weekly magazine, *Young India,* of August 6, 1925, "I turn to the *Bhagavad-Gita,* and find a verse to comfort me; and I immediately begin to smile in the midst of overwhelming sorrow." Mahadev Desai, for many years the Mahatma's secretary, testifies that "every moment of Gandhi's life is a conscious effort to live the message of the *Gita.*" Gandhi called it his "spiritual reference book."

The *Bhagavad-Gita* or Celestial Song is an exquisite poem of seven hundred stanzas, in the original Sanskrit, about the science and practice of yoga. Written by one person some time, according to scholars, between the fifth and second centuries B.C., the *Gita* is a battlefield conversation between its hero, Krishna, who is worshipped in India as a god, and Arjuna, the chief of a faction in a famous civil war. "Krishna," says Sir Sarvapalli Radhakrishnan, the Hindu philosopher, "is the human embodiment of Vishnu," the Supreme God.

The orthodox Hindu interpretation of the *Gita* as a divine summons to caste obligation and killing was repugnant to Gandhi and even when he first read the book in London in 1888-89 he called it an allegory in which the battlefield is the soul and Arjuna, man's higher impulses struggling against evil.

There are yogis who meditate and yogis who act. The yogi of action is the karma yogi. Mahatma Gandhi was a karma yogi. In a comment on the *Gita*, Gandhi defined the perfect karma yogi: "He is a devotee who is jealous of none, who is a fount of mercy, who is without egotism, who is selfless, who treats alike cold and heat, happiness and misery, who is ever forgiving, who is always contented, whose resolutions are firm, who has dedicated mind and soul to God, who causes no dread, who is not afraid of others, who is free from exultation, sorrow and fear, who is pure, who is versed in action yet remains unaffected by it, who renounces all fruit, good or bad, who treats friend and foe alike, who is untouched by respect or disrespect, who is not puffed up by praise, who does not go under when people speak ill of him, who loves silence and solitude, who has a disciplined reason. Such devotion is inconsistent with the existence at the same time of strong attachments."

Gandhi summarized it in one word: "Desirelessness."

Desirelessness, or Hindu renunciation, it has been

argued, leads to personal indifference and passivity and national poverty and stagnation. Gandhi contended, on the contrary, that to act while renouncing interest in the fruits of action is the best road to success. "He who is ever brooding over result," he wrote, "often loses nerve in the performance of duty. He becomes impatient and then gives vent to anger and begins to do unworthy things; he jumps from action to action, never remaining faithful to any. He who broods over results is like a man given to the objects of senses; he is ever-distracted, he says good-by to all scruples, everything is right in his estimation and he therefore resorts to means fair and foul to attain his end."

Renunciation, if one is capable of it, creates the inner peace and poise necessary to achieve real lasting results, even material results, untainted by ugly means. For the exceptional practitioner of self-denial a special prize is in store. The yogi's highest recompense is to become so firmly united with God after death that he need never again return to the status of migrating mortal man. Several times in his life Gandhi expressed the hope not to be born anew.

Mahatmas are rare. Desirelessness is an ideal to which few in India or anywhere attain or even aspire, but the young Hindu, reciting the *Bhagavad-Gita* several times a month, indeed more frequently perhaps, at home or in the temple, becomes aware of its injunctions and may be inspired, on the threshold of life, to ponder the purpose of life. Gandhi undoubtedly did, and it affected his entire future.

FROM: GANDHI — *His Life and Message for the World.* Copyright 1954 by Louis Fischer and published as a MENTOR BOOK by the New American Library of World Literature, Inc.

The Mentor Philosophers